ELIZABETH
THE QUEEN MOTHER

ELIZABETH
THE QUEEN MOTHER

—

1900–2002

GRANIA FORBES

PAVILION

'To Mark, Edward, Matthew and George'

First published in Great Britain in 1999 by
PAVILION BOOKS LIMITED
A member of **Chrysalis** Books plc
64 brewery road, London N7 9NT
This revised edition published 2002

Text © Grania Forbes 1999, 2002
The moral right of the author has been asserted.

Designed by Nigel Partridge

A CIP catalogue record for this book is available from the
British Library.

ISBN 1 86205 416 9

Set in Centaur and Trajan

Colour reproduction by Colourpath, London
Printed and bound in Great Britain by
Bath Press Limited

1 3 5 7 9 10 8 6 4 2

This book may be ordered by post direct from the publisher.
Please contact the Marketing Department. But try your
bookshop first.

CONTENTS

———⊰⊱———

THE FAMILY TREE OF
ELIZABETH BOWES LYON AND GEORGE VI

Elizabeth Bowes Lyon was born into one of the most distinguished Scottish families, whose ancestry can be traced back to King Robert the Bruce. On George's side, the House of Windsor is shown here from the reign of Queen Victoria.

The Queen Mother waves to the crowd of supporters outside Clarence House,
London, on the day of her 101st birthday.

CHAPTER ONE

A SCOTTISH LASS

Below: St Paul's Walden Bury, the childhood home of the Queen Mother, and the magic wood where she played as a child.

The year was 1900, the dawning of a new era and yet vestiges of the previous century lingered on. The disgraced playwright Oscar Wilde lay dying in Paris, the obstinate Boers were soon to be trounced but not defeated at Ladysmith and Mafeking, the Australian Commonwealth was about to be proclaimed and Lily Langtry was about to be exposed by the American press as the Prince of Wales's mistress, as she played the part of a dissolute heiress in Washington. Strenuous efforts were being made to 'solve' the continuing Irish problem and the trade unions had decided to abandon the 'Liberals' and form their own 'Labour' party. Long-distance buses had started operating (the journey from London to Leeds took two days) and a new drink called Coca-Cola was launched.

Queen Victoria, who had come to the throne in 1837, still held sway at Buckingham Palace but, now aged eighty-one, she was beginning to fade. Her nerves, frail at the best of times, were further stretched when a fifteen-year-old anarchist made an attempt to shoot the Prince of Wales during a visit to Brussels.

Opposite: A portrait by Bertram Park which captures that allure which won the Queen Mother so many suitors. She was a great admirer of his work and sat regularly for him.

Into this changing world came a girl who was destined to achieve greatness comparable to the old Queen and, like her, become a beloved national institution. Her name was Elizabeth Angela Marguerite Bowes Lyon, the ninth of ten children born to the Earl and Countess of Strathmore. She arrived with the minimum of fuss on 4 August when the weather was so hot that horses were forced to wear straw hats and débutantes had to abandon that fashionable new dance, the 'cakewalk'.

Just where she was born has been the subject of much debate but modern historians now agree that it was in London and not, as previously supposed, at the family's Hertfordshire home, St Paul's Walden Bury. Indeed, in her passport, issued in 1921, her place of birth was clearly stated as London. The mystery arose because her father, a sweet-natured but absent-minded man, was six weeks late registering her birth and only dashed into nearby Hitchin to record her arrival at the Bury two days before her christening. He was fined 7s 6d for being so tardy. However, eighty years later, the Queen Mother proudly announced that she was born a Londoner and then refused to explain further saying, 'It is of no matter.'

Several theories have been put forward for the mix-up. One theory is that her mother, then aged thirty-eight, was advised by her doctors that it might be wise to book into a nursing home for the birth as it was seven years since her last pregnancy. At that time it was not the 'done thing' for aristocrats to use such places and it might have been decided that once the child was safely delivered, mother and baby would be discreetly driven to their country home.

Another possibility is that Elizabeth arrived rather suddenly as her mother motored down from London to St Paul's. This would account for a local doctor from Welwyn, whose practice lay on the route from the capital to the country, proudly telling his family that he was present at the birth and would explain his subsequent invitation to her wedding.

Perhaps the most probable explanation is that the baby's father simply could not face a hot and tiring journey to London to register the birth and chose instead to nip down the road to Hitchin. He may have felt that his little white lie was of no consequence and indeed it would not have been but for the fact that his youngest daughter would one day be Queen. Certainly Elizabeth's arrival did not cause a stir. Her paternal grandfather, the 13th Earl of Strathmore and Kinghorn, did not even mention her birth in his daily diary.

The baby was born into one of the oldest and most distinguished Scottish families. On her father's side, the Lyons could trace their ancestry back to the Picts who fought so valiantly against the Romans, and descended from King Robert the Bruce.

Above: A house party at St Paul's Walden Bury. Standing: Lord Elphinstone, Patrick, Lord Strathmore, Malcolm Lyon, James Stuart. Sitting: Elizabeth, Betty Cator, Dorothy, Lady Strathmore, May, Bettine Malcolm; Cecilia (the daughter of Patrick and Dorothy) is seated on the ground.

Above: The Queen Mother with her parents and brother David. Always a chatterbox, she has plenty to say while her beloved black satin spaniel, Peter, waits patiently at her side.

The Bowes part of the name arrived in the mid-eighteenth century when a Durham heiress married into the family. Her mother, Nina Cecilia Cavendish Bentinck, was equally grand. Had she been a boy, she would have become the 6th Duke of Portland.

However, for all their lineage, the Bowes Lyons were not a stuffy lot. Theirs was a large and happy tribe which consisted of May, who was seventeen when Elizabeth was born, followed by Patrick, Jock, Alexander, Fergus, Rose and Michael. When Elizabeth was twenty-one months old, David arrived to complete the family. Her eldest sister, Violet Hyacinth, had died of heart problems brought on by diphtheria aged eleven, seven years before Elizabeth was born.

Lady Strathmore was the keystone of the family, so admired and adored by all her children that she never needed to punish them. A gentle word of reproof was enough to shame them into obedience. As one of her daughters recalled, 'Mother was a very wonderful woman, very talented, very go-ahead and so upright. She had terrific sympathy: the young used to pour their troubles out to her and ask her for advice, often when they would not go to their own parents. She was extremely artistic. She sewed lovely embroidery, which she designed herself. She had an extremely good ear for music. She would go to a concert and listen to a piece of music, and then come back and play it perfectly.'

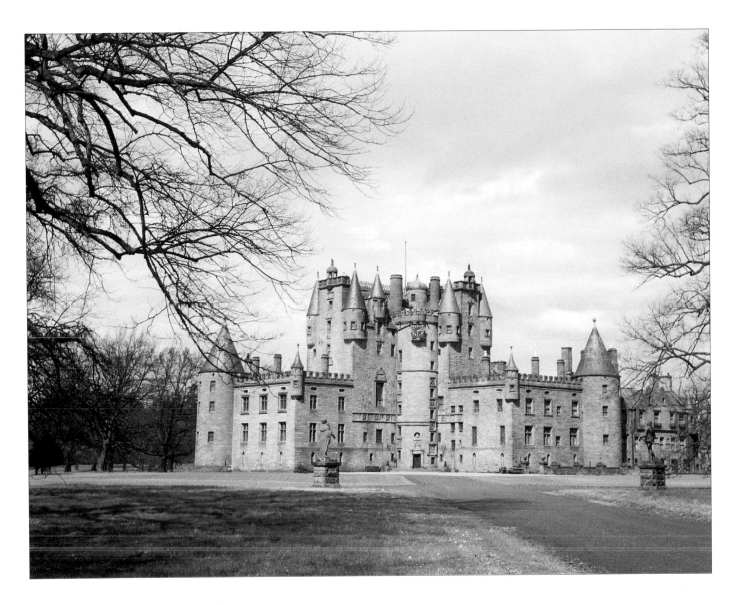

Lady Strathmore was not only adored by her children but also by the household servants. A housemaid, who later became Lady Elizabeth's dresser when the staff were hard pressed, remembers an occasion when she smashed a valuable antique. 'I was cleaning out the drawing-room after a weekend house party and moving the screens round the fireplace that kept the draughts away. What I didn't realize was that there was a precious vase on a plinth just behind one of them. Anyway, as I moved one of them, to clean under it, there was a sickening crash. I pulled it back and there was the vase in a thousand pieces,' recalls Miss Monty. 'Well, I

Above: Glamis Castle, the family's romantic and haunted Scottish stronghold which Elizabeth's father inherited when she was four. She and David were fond of pouring icy water from the topmost tower onto visitors waiting at the front door.

Below: Elizabeth, aged two, coolly surveys the world from her high chair. Her nanny described her as 'an exceptionally happy, easy baby, crawling early, running at thirteen months and speaking very young.'

Opposite: Elizabeth aged four with her adored 'bruver' David, three. The pair were inseparable and were nicknamed 'my two Benjamins' by their mother. Others found their pranks more impish and she was dubbed the 'merry mischief'.

thought I was going to get dismissed and when I was summoned by the butler to Lady Strathmore's room (she was ill at the time) I was certain of it. She was sitting propped up in bed. I thought, "Now I'm for it" but to my amazement, she put out her hand towards me. It was covered in beautiful diamond rings. She said: "I hear you've been in the wars, Mabel. I am so sorry. Accidents will happen. It was only a Ming." And that was it. I nearly fainted but that was just like her or so the others told me. I hadn't been there for very long, you see. She was the most wonderful employer and we all loved her.'

However, Lady Strathmore was no libertarian when it came to her offspring. She imbued them with the maxims normally found on the samplers children embroidered in Victorian times. 'Duty is the rent you pay for life,' was one of her favourites. Another was 'Life is for living and working at. If you find anything or anyone a bore, the fault is in yourself.' It was a motto that Elizabeth would carry with her for the rest of her life.

Like her husband, Lady Strathmore was deeply religious. Church parade and daily prayers were as much a part of daily life as eating or sleeping. It was this faith that enabled her to try to cope with the grief over the death of her eldest daughter, Violet, and later the demise of Alexander, who was killed by a brain tumour following a cricketing accident at Eton. Nevertheless, Lady Strathmore was not a conventional Victorian mother. Unlike other Countesses of her time, she refused to hire a wet nurse for her babies, preferring to feed them herself. Her offspring slept for the first eighteen months of their lives in a cot at her bedside and she supervised every detail of their daily lives. Although gregarious and a wonderful raconteuse, she was rarely absent from home and while undoubtedly loyal to the Crown, she scorned snobbery and the social round that endorsed it. She was once heard to quip that 'some hostesses feed royalty to their guests as zoo keepers feed

Above: Even as a toddler, Elizabeth had the knack of posing for the camera.

fish to seals.' She was also unusual in that, at a time when most aristocrats and royalty treated their children as third-class citizens to be given the plainest of everything, Lady Strathmore made sure hers had the best. This even extended to the nursery where, according to her granddaughter, Lady Mary Clayton, the décor could have graced the grandest drawing-room in the land. 'My grandmother was of the opinion that children, however small, should be surrounded by fine things so they would learn to love and appreciate them. The nursery at the Bury was no exception and had lovely furniture and beautiful paintings. I remember the walls were covered with Miacchis which were exquisite pictures of mythological legends or religious scenes. They were very like the illuminations in an old manuscript. The painter was a good friend of my great-grand-mother, Mrs Scott, and lived in Florence.'

Lady Strathmore also brought a touch of Tuscany to the high-lands of Scotland. Over ten years she created an Italian garden in the grounds of Glamis Castle where Elizabeth, nicknamed the 'merry mischief', and her 'bruver' liked to play. All this made a great impression on the young Elizabeth and throughout her life the Queen Mother not only had exquisite taste but an enthusi-astic passion for gardening.

Elizabeth's father was a much more down-to-earth character. His favourite garb was an old coat tied at the waist with a piece of twine and his favourite occupations were lopping trees and

Opposite: Elizabeth and David loved to play in the Italian garden which they helped their mother to create. The experience aroused a passion for horticulture which was never to leave the Queen Mother. Glamis can be seen in the background.

Above: Elizabeth, aged eight, with her faithful brother, David, at her side, learnt early the art of 'mixing'. Here she looks on as her mother, Lady Strathmore, talks to guests at a garden party at Glamis.

digging ditches. He was frequently mistaken by visitors for one of his farm labourers and offered a swig of whisky to keep out the cold. He also had the slightly eccentric habit of going out in the middle of the night to collect fallen branches which he would chop into kindling in his study. When asked about his nocturnal activities, he would reply that it was the only time he could get 'a little peace'.

Lord Strathmore shared his wife's passion for music. His own father had written choral works and trained his twelve offspring as a madrigal group. He loved to recite from the classics and was an expert on the Bible. He also never failed to complete the *Telegraph* crossword. His great passion, however, was cricket and

Opposite: Elizabeth in her dancing costume, made by her mother and copied from a Velázquez painting. She and David would perform the minuet, to the delight of visitors to the castle.

Opposite: *Elizabeth,*
aged seven, cradles an
armful of blossom, a
blue bow in her hair.
The picture is a family
favourite and shows her
early love of pearls.

games against local teams were taken seriously – particularly the annual needle-match against the Dundee Drapers. When he achieved a hat trick of three wickets against them, his jubilant team bought him a new Panama hat.

Such was the piety of Lord Strathmore's father that he had practically bankrupted the estate by building Episcopalian churches throughout Scotland. The consequence was that Elizabeth's father spent much of his lifetime paying off the debt and had to sell land. This meant that the family were not well off by the standards of the time and Lady Strathmore's account book shows what a careful housekeeper she was. Every item of expenditure, down to the last bar of soap, is recorded. Indeed, it used to be a joke among the tenants on the estate that when they heard shooting, they knew that a dinner party was planned at the Castle. 'They needed the game, you see, for the table,' explains old retainer Jock Scott.

It was in this Edwardian world that Elizabeth was brought up. When she was a month old, her mother employed Clara Cooper Knight, the daughter of a tenant farmer at Glamis, who was to serve generations of the Strathmore family. Always known as 'Allah', because it was the nearest that the children could get to pronouncing Clara, she was the archetypal nanny – gentle but firm, very professional, very loyal, extremely efficient and serene in even the most difficult circumstances. She also adored the children and they her. She describes the young Elizabeth as 'an exceptionally happy, easy baby, crawling early, running at thirteen months and speaking very young.' Soon Elizabeth's constant companion was her brother, David, and the two played together like twins. Raiding the larder and begging sweets from the cook were favourite occupations as was pouring 'boiling oil' from the top-most turret of Glamis, ninety feet up, onto unsuspecting visitors below. The 'oil' was in fact icy water but it had the desired effect. Other pranks included taking villagers 'hostage' until a ransom of sweets was paid or upsetting the chauffeur by putting a football under the front wheels of the family motor car. When the poor man engaged the clutch, there was a loud explosion which nearly gave him heart failure.

When down south at their Hertfordshire home, St Paul's Walden Bury, Elizabeth and David had a secret den in the old ruined brew house in the grounds. They found their hiding place while searching for a stray bantam and had christened it the Flea House for reasons that became only too apparent. It was there that they would skip their morning lessons to smoke the cigarettes and eat the chocolate they had acquired by devious means while a frantic Allah searched for them in vain. The older Strathmore children complained that their younger siblings 'got away with murder' and even the Countess had to admit a certain indulgence to her 'two Benjamins' as she nicknamed them. As she once sighed when faced with an implacable Elizabeth, 'I pity the man you marry because you are *so* determined.'

However, sometimes despite protest, what Mother said went. Guests had to be entertained and the pair – David dressed in a jester's costume bearing the Strathmore coat of arms and Elizabeth in a dress copied from a Velázquez painting – used to perform the minuet as their dancing teacher, Mr Neill, skipped ahead in his heavy brown boots playing the fiddle. The visitors found it enchanting but to the children it was embarrassing.

Like other young ladies of her generation, Lady Elizabeth, as she became after her father inherited the Strathmore title in 1904, was educated mainly at home. Initially it was Allah who taught her the basics of reading, writing and arithmetic but soon governesses were employed including Miss Laurel Gray. Lady Strathmore asked Miss Gray to keep an account book of the children's progress. 'When they were good, a good mark and a penny. And, of course, a bad mark was shocking,' she recalled. 'Elizabeth wasn't too good but she always got a good mark. She was naturally a good scholar. A bad mark made no difference to David. I was as strict as I could be but he was terrible!'

Elizabeth quickly learnt to read and at an early age 'devoured books'. Initially she liked stories about animals but soon moved on to tales of chivalry and adventure, passed down by her older brothers and sisters. History books particularly intrigued her and she was fascinated by atlases showing the different countries of the world. From the age of six, she and David had a series of French, and later German, governesses, and she was fluent in both languages by the age of ten. Also on her busy schedule were piano lessons and dance classes not to mention a personal art tutor. She had inherited her mother's musical ear and was the star performer at a school concert when she spent two terms at the Misses Birtwistle's Academy in London. Her ever-indulgent mother had sent her there partly as an experiment but also to cure her loneliness after her brother, David, was sent to preparatory school in Broadstairs. The loss of her companion hit her hard. As she wrote to a friend, 'David went off to school for the first time on Friday. I miss him horribly.'

However, Lady Strathmore decided that Elizabeth was better educated at home and more governesses arrived to continue her education. In June 1914, Lady Elizabeth sat the Oxford Preliminary Local Examination and passed all seven set subjects with flying colours. They were Arithmetic, English history, English, Geography, French, German and Drawing. A few weeks

Above: Elizabeth and David, in a jester's costume, with their dancing master, Mr Neill. He would skip ahead of them during a performance, playing the fiddle. He was an old family friend and entertained guests at Elizabeth's grandparents' golden wedding celebrations.

Above: As the First World War loomed, Elizabeth was already a sophisticated and mature young woman — and an accomplished hostess.

later, the First World War was declared as she sat watching the music hall on her fourteenth birthday — and her education effectively ended.

While Lady Elizabeth was being cosseted, some might even say spoilt, by her family and friends, her future husband, Prince Albert Frederick Arthur George, second son of the Duke of York and Princess Mary, later King George V and Queen Mary, was having a very thin time of it.

Born in 1895 on that dreaded day of mourning, 14 December, the date when both Queen Victoria's adored Consort, Prince Albert, and her beloved daughter, Princess Alice, had met their maker, it was not an auspicious start. Even his christening had to be postponed because of the death of his great-uncle, Prince Henry of Battenburg, spouse of the Queen's adored youngest daughter, and the forerunner of men who would shape the future of the British monarchy (his great-nephew was Lord Louis Mountbatten).

Despite the Duke of York's trepidation at telling his grandmother the news, 'Gan-gan' reacted favourably saying, 'I have a feeling it may be a blessing for the dear little boy and may be looked upon as a gift from God.' He further ingratiated himself by offering to call the infant Albert and making Queen Victoria his godmother. She was so delighted that she commissioned a bust of his saintly great-grandfather, Prince Albert to be made as a christening present and wrote, 'It is a great satisfaction to us all that it should be a second boy and I need not say how *delighted* I am that my great wish – viz. that the little one born on that sad anniversary should have the dear name of *Albert*.' To her disgust, her own heir (Albert Edward), although always called Bertie, had made it plain that he would never be called King Albert the First and eventually became King Edward VII.

She was also aware, as was the leading newspaper of the day, the *Morning Advertiser*, that 'an heir and a spare' was essential given her own experience. While her eldest son, however much she disapproved of him, might still be alive, she had lost the next heir – her grandson Albert Victor – who died of pneumonia soon after his engagement to Princess Mary of Teck. The Queen, finding no other suitable bride, married Mary (who was known as Princess May) to Albert's younger brother, the Duke of York, who later became King George V. As Frances Donaldson comments in her biography of Edward VIII, 'It was a matter of chance, though a happy one, that the Duke of York was, by character and temperament, the more suitable both for the Crown and to the tastes and affections of his future wife.'

For their first seventeen years together, Prince Albert's parents lived in York Cottage on the

Below: Prince Albert Frederick Arthur George, the second son of the Duke and Duchess of York, aged eighteen months. He was always known as Bertie and later became King George VI.

Above: The Duke and Duchess of York, later King George V and Queen Mary, pose proudly with their eldest son Prince Edward. However, David, as he was known, was to prove a great disappointment to his parents and eventually abdicated to marry American divorcée Wallis Simpson.

Sandringham estate in Norfolk. Described as 'a glum little villa similar to those found on the outskirts of London', it was a rabbit warren of very small rooms and narrow passages. It constantly stank of stale cabbage, there were not enough bathrooms and the Duke of York himself commented that he supposed the servants must sleep in the trees.

The Duke was by nature a martinet, neat, punctual and hardworking. He led the life of a traditional country squire and spent most of his time shooting. He was irrationally proud of his family and the slightest infringement of his rules, real or imagined,

would throw him into an apoplexy of rage. He was not above putting his boys over his knee to smack them and even his 'adored May' got the rough edge of his tongue, silently leaving the table when she could stand his rudeness no longer.

On his fifth birthday, Bertie received a letter from his father. It said, 'Now that you are five years old, I hope you will always try to & be obedient & do at once what you are told, as you will find it will come much easier to you the sooner you begin. I always tried to do this when I was your age & found it made me much happier.' There was no birthday present, no birthday party – not even a card.

Bertie's mother was a strong and purposeful woman but lacked the maternal instinct. By

nature extremely reserved, she was incapable of showing overt affection and left the upbringing of her three eldest children, Princess Mary having been born a year after Bertie, to a nurse. The woman is widely described as 'sadistic and incompetent' and ended her days in an asylum though not before she had made the royal children's lives a misery for many years. Mrs Christina Stringer was the maternity nurse at Sandringham and she told her daughter-in-law of the horrors she witnessed at York Cottage. 'She told me that the nurse was so harsh and so strict that the children had a worse life than any of the village young-sters. She used to hit them with a big rod for no reason at all and never cared for them at all. They weren't even properly fed,' says Mrs Mabel Stringer. 'She was particularly cruel to Prince Albert because he had a stutter and had temper tantrums but the more she hit him with the rod, the more difficult he became. She was dreadful to him. According to my mother-in-law, when she vented her anger on him with the rod, he would just cower away and hide himself.'

Her favourite charge was David, later King Edward VIII and the Duke of Windsor, but she was so jealous of him possibly forming any sort of attachment with his parents that she would twist or pinch his arm so hard that he would scream in agony when he entered the drawing-room. This led his mother to believe that her son could not stand the sight of her and the children were hastily bundled back to the nursery. 'The sobbing and bawling this treatment invariably invoked understandably puzzled, worried and finally annoyed my parents,' the Duke of Windsor recalled in his memoirs. The nurse's reign of terror only ended when a brave nursery footman reported her activities to the Duke. To their astonishment, he and the Duchess discovered that the woman had not had a day off in three years and that their chil-dren were suffering from rickets, a disease normally associated with the half-starved children of slum dwellers. Later Bertie had to wear splints to correct his knock knees and his stammer wors-

Above: The little
Princes watching the
Proclamation at St
James's that would
make their father King
George V. The Duke of
Gloucester stands
between Bertie (left)
and David (right).

ened when a private tutor forced him to write with his right hand.

However, the Duchess of York's sense of fun surfaced when the highly repressive influence of her husband was removed. 'When he used to go banging away for a week or two on some shoot in the Midlands, and my mother would never go to those things, we used to have the most lovely time with her alone – always laughing and joking down at Frogmore or wherever we might be – she was a different human being away from him,' remembered the Duke of Windsor. When the boys served their French master tadpoles on toast as a savoury, their mother was highly amused. 'My father would have been furious. She liked that sort of thing when she was alone with us.' Another bonus was that Bertie was a natural athlete and shone at sport. He out-played his brother on the golf course and hunted with the West Norfolk Hounds. He learnt to skate when the lakes at Sandringham froze and was a star at football and cricket. He and David would organize teams to play the local boys from the estate.

Despite a struggle with maths, Bertie passed his examination to Osborne and entered the Royal Naval College just after his fourteenth birthday in January 1909, a year before his father was crowned King George V. He found the life hard and lonely and within six months he was sent home with whooping cough. Although he came bottom (or very nearly) of his class, he entered Dartmouth two years later. Within a month both he and David caught mumps and measles, and their condition was sufficiently severe to warrant bulletins in the medical journal, *The Lancet.*

Desperate to serve his country, Prince Albert was thwarted by ill health, which plagued him throughout the First World War. First he was rushed ashore to have his appendix removed, then he experienced acute stomach pains and had to be given a desk job at the Admiralty – a sinecure where he became bored and restless. Finally his pleas to be returned to his ship were heard but within three months he was back on the hospital ship and declared unfit for active service. Despite protests from his father, it was not until May 1916 that Bertie, debilitated and depressed, returned to his ship, the *Collingwood.* However, his moment of glory was at hand. The Battle of Jutland was about to begin and at last he was 'able to get at the enemy'. He describes it vividly.

'I was in a turret and watched most of the action through one of the trainer's telescopes as we were firing by Director, when the turret is trained in the working chamber and not in the gun house. At the commencement I was sitting on top of a turret and had a very good view of the proceedings. I was up there during a lull, when a German ship started firing at us, and one salvo "strad-dled" us. We at once returned fire. I was distinctly startled and jumped down the hole in the top of the turret like a shot rabbit! I didn't try the experience again … My impressions were very different to what I expected. I saw visions of the masts going over the side and funnels hurtling through the air etc. In reality none of these things happened and we are still quite as sound as we were before. No one would know to look at the ship that we had been in action. It was certainly a great experience to have been

Opposite: Bertie, aged eighteen, at the outbreak of the First World War. Although plagued by ill health, he fought gallantly at the Battle of Jutland. As his official biographer comments, 'In a single afternoon, he passed into the full dignity of manhood.'

Left: The outbreak of war was announced on the Queen Mother's fourteenth birthday. She was having a birthday treat at the music hall when she and her family first heard the news.

Above and right: A fever of nationalism gripped the nation and Elizabeth's four older brothers, like so many others, were quick to join up. 'It will all be over by Christmas', was the confident prediction.

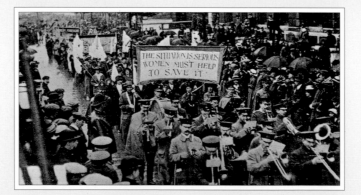

Below: This recruitment poster belies what these brave young men were to face. They saw the war as an exciting adventure but many were never to see home again.

Right: General Haig addresses
his troops. After the war was
over his leadership qualities
were questioned.

Above: A lone soldier walks
along the Amiens to St Quentin
Road, all his comrades gone. The
'lost generation' still lie where
they fell, in the poppy fields of
France and Belgium.

Right: The terrible slaughter.
The Queen Mother's brother,
Fergus, was killed at the Battle
of Loos in 1915. Her nephew
John, Lord Glamis, was killed
in action during the Second
World War.

through and it shows that we are at war and that the Germans can fight if they like.'

Having finally seen action in the front line, Prince Albert's confidence rose and he was able to brag to his older brother, 'When I was on top of the turret, I never felt any fear of shells or anything else. It seems curious but all sense of danger and everything else goes except the one longing to deal death in every possible way to the enemy.' In a later letter to David, he is in more philosophical mode. 'In a war on this scale, of course, we must have casualties and lose ships & men, but there is no need for everyone at home to bemoan their loss when they are proud to die for their country. They don't know what war is, several generations have come and gone since the last great battles.'

As Prince Albert's official biographer, Sir John Wheeler-Bennett, notes: 'In a single summer afternoon, he passed into the full dignity of manhood.' Sadly that was the end of Bertie's war.

Below: Elizabeth proudly wears her nurse's uniform on the steps of Glamis which was turned into a hospital during the First World War.

A duodenal ulcer was diagnosed and, after several periods of enforced rest, he underwent a successful operation in November 1917. The following year he was transferred to the Royal Naval Air Service in France, just two weeks before the Armistice was declared.

While Bertie was battling the Boche and his chronic ill health, Lady Elizabeth had been just as busy tending the sick and injured at Glamis Castle. No sooner had war been declared than her brothers joined up – Patrick, Jock and Fergus serving with the Black Watch, and Michael with the Royal Scots. It was also a time for weddings. On 17 September at Buxted in Sussex, Fergus married Lady Christian Dawson-Darmer and a week later the family rushed north to Scotland for Jock's marriage to Fenella Hepburn-Stuart-Forbes-Trefusis. Patrick was already married to

Above: Some of the 1,500 wounded soldiers who passed through the castle. Elizabeth would run errands for them, cheat at poker and join in bloody rat hunts in the crypt.

Lady Dorothy Osborne, the daughter of the Duke of Leeds, and Michael, being only twenty, was considered too young to contemplate matrimony.

The nuptials over, Lady Elizabeth, with her mother and sister, Rose, headed for Glamis where the castle was being converted into a convalescent hospital. Red Cross volunteers helped them move beds into the dining-room and billiard-room in readiness for the wounded but Lady Strathmore insisted that as little furniture as possible be displaced as she wished to make the castle homely. She instructed her family and staff that the soldiers should be treated as 'honoured guests' and made to feel welcome. As Lady Elizabeth told her biographer, Lady Cynthia Asquith, 'During these first few months we were busy knitting, knitting, knitting and making shirts for the local battalion, the 5th Black Watch. My chief occupation was crumbling up tissue paper until it was so soft that it no longer crackled to put into the linings of sleeping bags. Lessons were quite neglected.'

The first of the wounded arrived from Dundee Royal Infirmary in December 1914 while Rose was training to be a nurse at Bow Hospital in London, so many of her responsibilities fell to Lady Elizabeth. Above all, she carried out errands and was forever running up the mile-long drive to the village to buy tobacco, cigarettes and sweets for the men. She took photographs to send to their families and helped them write letters home as well as taking them on at poker and billiards. There were even noisy and bloody rat hunts in the crypt. The war-shattered veterans took the little girl to their hearts and a battered autograph book from those days survives. One entry speaks for all. It reads,

Below: For many of the wounded, their stay at Glamis was one of the happiest times of their lives and they continued to correspond with Elizabeth and her mother for many years after the conflict.

'May the owner of this book be
Hung, Drawn & Quartered.
"Yes."
Hung in Diamonds, Drawn in a Coach and Four.
And, Quartered in the Best House in the Land.'

W.H. Harrop of the 8th Seaforths little knew how prophetic he was.

In September 1915, Fergus returned to Glamis to celebrate his first wedding anniversary and see his baby daughter for the first time. Days later he returned to France where he was killed in action at the Battle of Loos. The whole family were grief-stricken but Lady Strathmore took the death particularly badly. For a while the running of the castle hospital was left to Lady Elizabeth and her sister, Rose, who had returned from London.

In May 1916, as Bertie was fighting valiantly at the Battle of Jutland, Lady Elizabeth was a bridesmaid when Rose married William Spencer Leveson Gower at St James's Church, Piccadilly. Although Rose returned to Glamis for brief periods thereafter, responsibility for the hospital fell heavily on Lady Elizabeth's shoulders. She was also anxious about her beloved mother and would wait nervously on the castle steps for the postman – just in case any more bad news arrived. And arrive it did. On 3 May 1917 Lord Strathmore telegraphed Rose, who was in London with her mother and expecting her husband home on leave, to break the news to his wife. His telegram from Glamis read: 'Michael missing April 28. War Office will wire further news. Tell mother they say not mean necessarily killed or wounded.' However, hope began to fade as strenuous enquiries failed to locate Michael's whereabouts. Only his youngest brother, David, who appeared to be gifted with second sight, was adamant that he was alive.

David Cecil, an old family friend, recalled a conversation he had with the fifteen-year-old. 'He lunched with me one day, and I pointed out to him that he should not wear coloured clothes and a coloured tie so soon after his brother's death. "Michael is not dead," protested David. "I have seen him twice. He is in a big house surrounded by fir trees. He is not dead, but I think he is very ill, because his head is tied up in a cloth."' David was right. Michael was a prisoner of war in Germany, where he remained until his release in 1919.

Above: The quick-thinking Elizabeth saved the castle from ruin when the central keep at Glamis caught fire in September 1916. The drawing-room and chapel were badly damaged by water and scorch marks can still be seen in the door leading to the roof.

Another drama also befell the Bowes Lyon family during the First World War. In September 1916 the central keep of the castle caught fire while the soldiers were out at the cinema. Lady Elizabeth promptly rang for help from the Dundee and Forfar fire brigades as well as the local Glamis station. She and David then set about organizing everyone into a chain, passing buckets and jugs of water. When a large water tank in the roof burst, they managed to divert the flow away from the drawing-room and rescued much of the valuable furniture, pictures and antiques. Lady Elizabeth's resourcefulness was credited with saving the castle from burning to the ground and she was toasted with 'Highland Honours' in every house and cottage for miles around. As the local paper, the *Dundee Courier*, put it, Lady Elizabeth 'was a veritable heroine in the salvage work she performed even within the fire zone.'

Although the war ended in November 1918, it was not until the following year that the hospital at Glamis finally waved goodbye to the last of the soldiers. Many never forgot the kindness they had received from the young Lady Elizabeth and continued to write to her for years afterwards. However, that was for later; now a mature eighteen-year-old, it was time for Lady Elizabeth to have some fun.

Opposite: The portrait that explains why Elizabeth was the most sought after débutante of her time. When her engagement was announced, the gentlemen's clubs were said to be 'in gloom.'

Right: The exquisite miniature of Elizabeth that her mother, Lady Strathmore, gave as a wedding gift to Bertie, Duke of York. It was to be his most treasured possession.

CHAPTER TWO

FAMILY FIRST

Opposite: An Adams portrait of the Queen Mother with her young daughters, the Queen (left) and Princess Margaret Rose. So close were they that 'if you crossed one, you crossed them all'. Some people found this out to their cost.

Right: Bertie, the eligible bachelor. He was tall and athletic with fair hair and blue eyes. He played championship tennis at Wimbledon and was a nifty dancer.

The Armistice found Prince Albert cooling his heels in the comfort of the British Embassy in Paris with his old friend, that 'perfect topper', Surgeon-Lieutenant Louis Greig, whom he had first met while a cadet at Osborne. During the four years of the war, the Prince had only managed to serve his country for twenty-two months and it was therefore thought politic that he should stay in France for a while to deflect any potential criticism from those who had lost loved ones in the conflict. As his older brother, David, wrote to their mother, Queen Mary, 'Bertie can be far more use in this way than sitting in England where he has spent most of the war, not that this was his fault! But by remaining with the armies till peace is signed, he will entirely erase any of the unfair questions some nasty people asked last year as to what he was doing, you will remember.'

Bertie spent Christmas away from the rest of the family at a Spa in Belgium where no doubt it was hoped that the curative waters would further improve his health. In the spring, he

represented the King at the victory celebrations in Brussels, his first major royal engagement.

It was during the festivities that Louis, the Prince's private secretary, bumped into James Stuart, who was hanging around waiting for his men to be demobilized and was the younger brother of an old friend. John Stuart and Louis went back a long way. They had been at Osborne and Dartmouth together and Louis knew James slightly. Since he and Bertie were almost of an age, Louis asked the young Major to show the Prince around and give him a good time. They went to the theatre, dined at the finest restaurants and took in the sights. It has even been suggested by some that the Prince lost his virginity at this time, which given James's sophistication and fondness for the company of women, might not be surprising.

As James recalled in his autobiography: 'He [Prince Albert] was young and did not want to stay in the Palace all the time. Thus, a few of us used to organize small parties and dances at The Merry Grill for the entertainment of the young Prince. We had a great deal of fun and I got to know the Prince quite well.' The Merry Grill was a smart restaurant and night-club, frequented by James who 'woke the place up' on New Year's Eve by bringing in a couple of his pipers. 'We had a lot of fun in Brussels and I grew to love the place. The small restaurants provided excellent food and Burgundy, but it was expensive and I soon found to my horror that, in a few weeks, I had spent all my war savings for four years.'

The Brussels encounter was to prove a turning point. When it was decided that Bertie should go up to Cambridge University and needed an equerry, Louis' thoughts naturally turned to James. The penniless third son of the Earl of Moray, having tired of studying for a legal career, was only too happy to accept a post in the Royal Household.

Meanwhile, Lady Elizabeth had just turned nineteen and was emerging as one of the prettiest débutantes of her generation, having been presented at Court at Holyroodhouse Palace during the King and Queen's summer stay in Edinburgh. She joined the normal round of parties, dances and outings to the Henley Royal Regatta and the Ascot race meeting. The family's London home at 20 St James's Square was the scene of almost nightly dinner parties and chambermaids made a brisk living passing on billets-doux from a host of admirers.

Weekends were spent at St Paul's Walden Bury where tennis, cricket and croquet occupied the 'bright young things' whenever they were not slipping off for quiet walks in the house's magnificent grounds, which were dotted with statuary, pavilions and ponds. Otherwise the group moved from one great house to another for weekend house parties. August found them in Scotland for shooting and the Forfar Ball where Lady Elizabeth never lacked dance partners. James, who had been at Eton with her brother Michael and served with him in the Royal Scots, was invited over to Glamis in the summer of 1919 and a year later Bertie followed, naturally accompanied by his equerry.

Mabell, Countess of Airlie, a close friend and neighbour of Lady Strathmore and lady-in-waiting to Queen Mary, said of Lady Elizabeth, 'Her radiant vitality and a blending of gaiety, kindness and sincerity made her irresistible to men.' Her dancing was so admired that she was awarded the accolade of 'best dancer in London'. Although the pair had met at a children's party, when

Above: Bertie and the great heiress Miss Edwina Ashley out pheasant shooting in 1920. She later married Earl Mountbatten of Burma, Prince Philip's uncle.

she was five and he ten, it was not until May 1920 that Lady Elizabeth caught Bertie's eye. She was dancing with James at a ball held by Lord and Lady Farquhar in Grosvenor Square. He called his equerry over and asked to be introduced. As he confided to Lady Airlie, he had fallen in love that evening 'although he did not realize it until later'.

However, the Prince had stiff competition. Despite a chronic shortage of suitable young men after the devastation of the First World War, Lady Elizabeth was surrounded by eligible suitors. There was Prince Paul of Yugoslavia, a close friend of her brother, Michael, at Oxford University, who was so keen to win her hand that, according to servants, he spent hours ingratiating himself with her mother, Lady Strathmore, hoping that she would persuade her daughter to accept his proposal. There was Lord Gage, immensely rich and the owner of Firle Place, a magnificent Tudor mansion in Sussex. 'Poor Gage is desperately fond of her,' noted the diarist Sir Henry 'Chips' Channon. 'In vain, for he is far too heavy, too Tudor and squirearchical for so rare and patrician a creature as Elizabeth.' Both the Earl of Airlie's older sons were smitten, the younger Brucie wooing her by dancing on table tops while playing the ukelele. Another faithful admirer was Sir Arthur Penn, twelve years her senior, who remained one of her most trusted friends; he served as her treasurer all his life and poignantly died the day before he was due to retire.

And then, of course, there was James. The Prince's equerry was a man of dashing good looks who had led a similarly adventurous life. He had run away from school to join up, while under age, at the beginning of the war and had distinguished himself on the battlefield, winning one Military Cross at the Battle of the Somme and another at the Battle of Arras. Described as 'drop down dead handsome', he never had to make the slightest effort to attract women. His take-it-or-leave-it attitude was irresistible and a raised eyebrow or a half smile had them captivated. James was also extremely witty and enjoyed nothing more than rather

Opposite: Life for the 'bright young things' was one endless round of parties. Elizabeth got so exhausted that her mother had to insist she was in by 2 am every night.

risqué banter, particularly with a pretty girl. He loved to tease and be teased, a trait he shared with Lady Elizabeth. The pair were increasingly seen together, particularly after James broke off his engagement to Elfie Finlayson, the daughter of a prosperous Glasgow trader. Everyone wondered if they would marry.

Meanwhile, Queen Mary had noted her younger son's interest in the beautiful débutante. During a carriage drive, she commented to Lady Airlie, 'I have discovered that he [Bertie] is very much attracted to Lady Elizabeth Bowes Lyon. He's always talking about her. She seems a charming girl but I don't know her very well.' 'I have known her all my life, and could say nothing but good of her,' replied her lady-in-waiting. It was now understood that she would act as royal marriage broker and as she relates, 'Soon after that the Duke and Lady Elizabeth started dropping in at my flat, on various pretexts, always separately but each talked of the other. She was frankly doubtful, uncertain of her feelings, and afraid of the public life which would lie ahead of her as the King's daughter-in-law. The Duke's humility was touching. He was deeply in love.'

Lady Airlie's counsel to Lady Elizabeth was that love 'would grow' with marriage. However, when Bertie proposed in the spring of 1921, he was refused. Lady Airlie wrote to Lady Strathmore that 'the Duke looked so disconsolate. I do hope he will find a nice wife who will make him happy.' Lady Elizabeth's mother replied, with some prescience, 'I like him so much and he is a man who will be made or marred by his wife.'

Elizabeth and Bertie remained good friends and continued to see each other as yet another season progressed. Gradually their friends married. Lady Lavinia Spencer and Lord Annaly, Helen Cecil and the King's private secretary Alec Hardinge, and Mollie Lascelles and the Earl of Dalkeith. Bertie remained adamant that if Lady Elizabeth would not have him, he would marry no one else. The Queen decided to travel north to judge Lady Strathmore's youngest daughter for herself. Lady Strathmore had

Right: Queen Mary, who fell under Elizabeth's spell after visiting Glamis and announced that she was 'the one girl who could make Bertie happy.' She then set about making sure that his main rival, James Stuart, was removed from the scene.

been ill for some time so it was Elizabeth who was waiting on the steps of Glamis to greet the royal party as they drew up on 9 September 1921. As ever, she was relaxed and charming and impressed Queen Mary with her poise and knowledge of history, something very dear to the old lady's heart. By the time she left, after a guided tour of the castle and a delicious tea, she was convinced that Lady Elizabeth was 'the one girl who could make Bertie happy'.

Drastic action was now needed. The mothers put their heads together and it was decided that it was time for James to go away for a while. So in the early days of 1922, he was dispatched to the oil fields of Oklahoma to be a rigger. By the time he returned, Lady Elizabeth had married Bertie and become the Duchess of York. In any case Lady Strathmore had decided that he was not a suitable match for her youngest daughter, given his wild ways and his broken engagement. He had no money of his own and nor had she, being the ninth child and fourth daughter of an Earl still up to his ears in debt. Although greatly distinguished later in life, at that stage James showed no signs of earning a living. As he was fond of saying himself, 'There is no point in marrying for love for love does not last but money does.' Instead he married where money was, Lady Rachel Cavendish, the fourth daughter of the Duke of Devonshire, on Elizabeth's twenty-third birthday, 4 August 1923. A solicitor drew up the marriage contract and according to the jilted Elfie's daughter, Lady Rachel proved to be just the sort of wife he wanted. 'She was beautiful, she was rich, and she was the most marvellously loyal and tolerant wife that any philanderer could have hoped to have.' Moreover, Lady Elizabeth had got his measure. She had noticed his roving eye during the Ascot race meeting of 1921 and considered him, for all his charm, unsuitable husband material.

The way was now clear for Bertie and he pursued Lady

Above: Elizabeth and Bertie in the woods at St Paul's Walden Bury in Hertfordshire where his proposal of marriage was finally accepted. 'He is the luckiest of men', wrote the diarist 'Chips' Channon when he heard the news.

Elizabeth with the same persistent obstinacy that had seen him through so many troubles earlier in his life. In February his sister, Princess Mary, married Viscount Lascelles and Lady Elizabeth was one of the bridesmaids. Intimate dinner parties followed at the home of the Hon Mrs Greville and the shooting season again found Bertie at Glamis. This time 'Chips' Channon was also among the house party. As he records in his diary, 'One rainy afternoon, we were sitting about and I pretended I could read cards, and I told Elizabeth Lyon's fortune and predicted a great and glamorous royal future. She laughed, for it was obvious that the Duke of York was much in love with her.' After the visit, Bertie wrote to his mother, 'The more I see of her, the more I like her.'

On 5 January 1923 the *Daily News* thought they had a scoop when they erroneously announced in banner headlines 'A Scottish

Bride for the Prince of Wales ... An Official Announcement Imminent.' Bertie was furious and issued a denial. Down at Firle, staying with Lord Gage, Lady Elizabeth was teased. As 'Chips' Channon reported, 'The evening papers have announced her engagement to the Prince of Wales. So we all bowed and bobbed and teased her, calling her "Ma'am": I am not sure that she enjoyed it. It couldn't be true, but how delighted everyone would be! She certainly has something on her mind. She is more gentle, lovely and exquisite than any woman alive, but this evening I thought her unhappy and *distraite*. I longed to tell her I would die for her, although I am not in love with her.'

Eight days later, at her Hertfordshire home, St Paul's Walden Bury, Lady Elizabeth and Prince Albert skipped church and went for a walk in the woods. Bertie proposed again and this time she accepted. His delighted parents received the telegram they had so long awaited. It simply said, 'All right Bertie.'

The official announcement two days later surprised 'Chips' Channon, among others. 'I was so startled and almost fell out of bed when I read the Court Circular. We have all hoped, waited, so long for this romance to prosper, that we had begun to despair that she would ever accept him ... He is the luckiest of men, and there is not a man in England today who

Below: Elizabeth with her father, the Earl of Strathmore, after her engagement was announced. She told friends she felt very happy but 'loathed' the press attention.

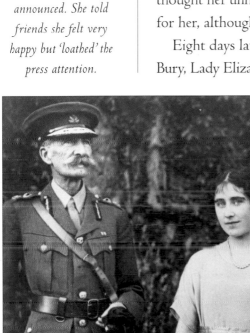

Above: One of the many official portraits that appeared in commemorative issues of the newspapers up and down the country when the engagement was officially announced.

Above: Elizabeth and Bertie just before their wedding at Westminster Abbey. The pair were showered with gifts and congratulations and had to employ extra staff to deal with all the messages of goodwill.

doesn't envy him. The clubs are in gloom.'

The wedding was set for 26 April and an engagement ring of a sapphire flanked by two diamonds was specially made. Lady Elizabeth based herself at the family's new London house, 17 Bruton Street, as congratulations and presents poured in. She admitted to friends feeling very happy but 'loathed' the press attention. Perhaps to silence them, she innocently gave her one and only newspaper interview. A gentle admonition came from the Palace and the mistake was never repeated. The King and Queen were delighted with her. 'Elizabeth is with us now, so well brought up, a great addition to the family,' wrote Bertie's mother approvingly.

The Queen gave her a diamond and sapphire necklace as a wedding present while the King chose a tiara and complete ensemble of diamonds and turquoises. From her father she received a diamond tiara and a necklace of pearls and diamonds. Bertie gave her a necklace of diamonds and pearls and she in turn gave him a dress watch chain of platinum and pearls.

No less precious was a gift from her own troupe of Girl Guides at Glamis, a silver pen and ink stand. The people of Forfar wrote to ask what gift would be appropriate. She replied with her natural sensitivity that, given 'everyone is feeling the pinch', she would treasure an illuminated address. No money, she insisted, was to be spent in these times of hardship.

Opposite: An engagement portrait of Elizabeth showing her unadorned beauty, just before she finally lost her fringe.

Below: Elizabeth first came to know the Royal Family through her association with the Girl Guides. Here she gratefully accepts a wedding present from her own Glamis troupe, a silver pen and ink stand.

Above: *Leaving her parents' home, 17 Bruton Street, for her wedding at Westminster Abbey on 26 April 1923. She left her gloves behind and a footman had to race her to the church and hand them to one of her bridesmaids in the nick of time.*

On the morning of her wedding, flanked by Lord Strathmore, she travelled in a state landau to Westminster Abbey, the first royal bride to be married there since 1382, when King Richard II took Princess Anne of Bohemia for his wife. Elizabeth's dress was medieval in style, of machine-made Nottingham lace with a veil of Flanders lace, lent by Queen Mary. The groom wore the uniform of a Group Captain of the Royal Air Force. In a spontaneous gesture, as she entered the Abbey, Lady Elizabeth placed her bouquet of York roses and white heather on the tomb of the Unknown Soldier. Her beloved brother Fergus, who had fallen so bravely in the service of his country, was not to be forgotten even on this most special of days. All other royal

Below: *The new Duchess of York poses with her husband before facing the daunting task of cutting the nine-feet-high wedding cake.*

52

brides have chosen to follow her example although they now keep their bouquet until they are on their way back from the altar. A request that some of the ceremony might be broadcast on the wireless was rejected on the grounds that 'disrespectful people might hear the service, perhaps even some of them sitting in public houses with their hats on.'

After the wedding breakfast at Buckingham Palace, where they faced the daunting task of cutting the nine-feet-high cake, the newlyweds left on honeymoon, first to Polesden Lacey in Surrey, the home of a mutual friend, and later to Glamis. Unfortunately the weather in Scotland was so bad that the new Duchess of York went down with whooping cough, which she later described as 'not a very romantic disease.'

Below: A family group. From left to right; the Earl of Strathmore, the Countess of Strathmore, the Duchess of York, the Duke of York, Queen Mary, King George V.

Above: The newlyweds leave on honeymoon, first to the home of a mutual friend and then to Glamis. In Scotland, the weather was so atrocious that the Duchess went down with whooping cough which she later described as 'not a very romantic disease.'

Below and opposite: Very much in love, the honeymoon couple have a round of golf before posing for the camera.

If Elizabeth had had her doubts about the marriage, they were to prove unfounded. As the wise Lady Airlie had predicted, love grew apace as the list of their official engagements mounted. The new Duchess's confidence in public rubbed off on her husband and he was further helped by the Australian speech therapist, Lionel Logue, who taught him a new way of breathing to correct his stammer.

When he had to make a speech, he now had the Duchess at his side mouthing the words he had to say and occasionally touching his hand for reassurance. As Bertie wrote from Balmoral to Mr Logue, he could even get his father to understand him. 'Up here I have been talking a lot with the King, and I have no trouble at all. Also, I can make him listen and I don't have to repeat everything over again.' In private, the Duchess used to try to make life as serene for him as possible. On evenings off, a supper tray would be sent up to the private sitting-room they shared and if the Duke was away from home, she wrote to him every day.

The Duchess even found a way of deflecting his nervous rages, known in the family as 'gnashes'. She would gently take his pulse and count, 'tick, tick, tick, one, two, three', which invariably made him smile. The normal cause of these upsets was her chronic unpunctuality. Like Bertie's grandmother, Queen Alexandra, who nearly missed her own Coronation because she was so late, 'the dear little Duchess' as she was known, could not turn up on

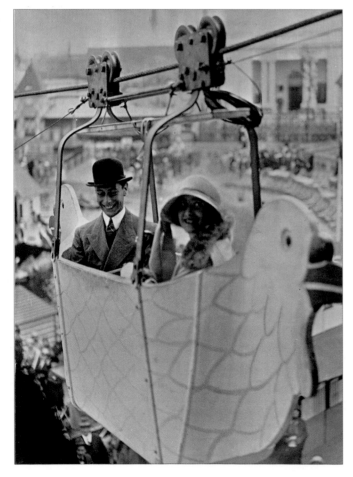

Below: the Duke and Duchess of York at the Wembley Exhibition in 1925. Her natural sense of fun and confidence in public rubbed off on her shy husband. With her at his side, official duties were no longer an ordeal.

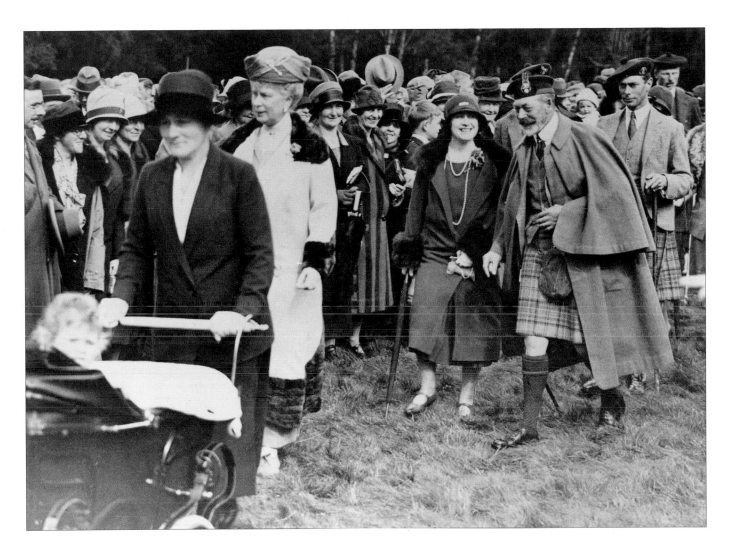

time. It was not unusual to find Bertie pacing up and down the corridor, muttering, 'Where *is* that damned woman?' She was even late for dinner with her father-in-law, something no one else would have dared to be. As the Duke cringed behind her, expecting an almighty blast from his father, his wife laughingly apologized. To everyone's astonishment, the King merely replied, 'Not at all, my dear. You are not late. I think we must have sat down a few minutes early.'

Elizabeth had no difficulty in getting on well with the King. She realized early on that his bark was worse than his bite and she became deeply fond of him. As she wrote to the royal physician after his death in 1936, 'I miss him dreadfully. Unlike his

Above: The Duchess of York and her father-in-law, King George V, share a joke at Balmoral in 1928. Unlike his own children, she was never afraid of him and when he died she admitted to missing him 'dreadfully'. Our present Queen can be seen in her pram leading the procession.

ELIZABETH: THE QUEEN MOTHER

own children I was never afraid of him, and in all the twelve years of having me as a daughter-in-law, he never spoke one unkind or abrupt word to me, and was always ready to listen and give advice on one's own silly little affairs. He was so kind and *dependable*! And when he was in a mood, he could be deliciously funny too!'

The couple's happiness was plain for all to see. As the diplomat Duff Cooper wrote to his wife after going to the theatre with them, 'The Duke and Duchess of York were there. They are such a sweet little couple and so fond of one another. They reminded me of us, sitting together in the box having private jokes, and in the interval when we were all sitting in the room behind the box they slipped out, and I found them standing together in a dark corner of the passage talking happily as we might. She affects no shadow of airs and graces.'

Their first home, when they returned to London from their honeymoon, was White Lodge in Richmond Park, formerly the home of Queen Mary and now the headquarters of the Royal Ballet School. It was large, cold, damp and ugly. The Duchess wrote to her mother begging her to send down some of her personal possessions from Glamis to make the place more homely. Despite having her belongings about her, the Duchess was frequently ill during the next year which greatly worried her husband. A bad bout of bronchitis doubled his anxiety and he was determined that his delicate bride would not endure another English winter. He arranged for a safari to East Africa over Christmas 1924. The trip lasted four months and they both returned to Britain rested and healthy. In August they left for Glamis and Balmoral, and to everyone's delight, the Duchess announced that she was expecting their first child.

On 19 November, an urgent message arrived from Sandringham to say that Queen Alexandra, the Queen Mother, had suffered a severe heart attack. During their bleak childhood, their grandmother had been their one source of affection and warmth, and David and Bertie hurried to her bedside.

Unfortunately, fog came down over East Anglia and by the time they arrived, the house was in darkness. They had lost their race to say goodbye. Queen Alexandra was dead.

On Wednesday, 21 April 1926, Elizabeth Alexandra Mary was born at twenty minutes to three in the morning at the Strathmore's London home, 17 Bruton Street. It was a difficult birth and a Caesarean section was necessary. The King and Queen hurried up from Windsor to see their baby granddaughter. Queen Mary noted that the new princess was 'a little darling with a lovely complexion and fair hair.' The christening took place in the private chapel at Buckingham Palace on 29 May and the baby was blessed with holy water from the River Jordan. 'Of course poor baby cried,' the Queen wrote in her diary. Apparently the efforts

Below: The Duchess of York proudly shows off her eldest daughter who was christened Elizabeth Alexandra Mary in the private chapel at Buckingham Palace on 29 May 1926.

of her grandmother, her mother and the Archbishop of York failed to still the child and it was only after she was handed back to her nurse, the Duchess's faithful old nanny Allah, that she was quietened. The solution, said the Press, lay in a bottle.

Their happiness now complete, the Duke and Duchess settled down to family life and found themselves a permanent home at 145 Piccadilly. However, they were not to enjoy their peace for long. When Lilibet, as the little Princess was nicknamed, was just eight months old, the royal couple were asked by the King to undertake a six-month tour of Australia and New Zealand. Despite the Duchess falling ill with tonsillitis during the early part of the trip, the tour was most definitely a triumph. As the Duke happily wrote to his father, 'I had to make three speeches the first morning … I had perfect confidence in myself and did not hesitate at all.'

Queen Mary took charge of the nursery and Allah and the Princess moved to Buckingham Palace. The Queen's cousin, Lady Mary Clayton, then aged nine, remembers afternoons there. 'Luckily my governess and Allah were great friends and I used to

be taken to Buckingham Palace to play with my cousin. I had always longed for a baby sister and she was absolutely sweet – delicious. If it was fine we used to play in the gardens and, if not, we would be round the fire playing games.'

She says Lilibet was a very good-humoured child and, as she grew older, would always 'listen to reason'. 'Occasionally she wouldn't answer but that was only because she was [pretending to be] a horse and couldn't.' However, there was one problem. Lilibet kept overhearing other nannies saying, 'Oh! You can't tell her off. She's a Princess' and this led her to believe that she could do no wrong,' recalls Lady Mary. 'One day we were playing cards with my mother and Lilibet was cheating. When she was told off,

Below: The Brownies turn out to welcome the Duchess of York during a visit to Stepney in 1933. The Duchess always had a great affection for the people of the East End.

she replied, "I can cheat if I want to, I'm a Princess." Well, we all started cheating and she saw that it was pointless to play a game if you cheated. And she never did it again.'

Meanwhile, Lilibet's parents busied themselves with an ever-increasing round of public duties; the Duke was heavily involved with everything from the Industrial Welfare Society to Dr Barnado's Homes while the Duchess concentrated on hospitals, child welfare and needlework. Whenever possible, they liked to carry out engagements together. August 1930 found the royal couple as usual ensconced at Glamis and on the twenty-first, as thunder and lightning rattled round the castle battlements, Princess Margaret Rose was born at twenty-two minutes past nine in the evening. Again it was a Caesarean birth. There was much rejoicing and a huge bonfire on Hunter's Hill, despite the down-pour, because she was the first royal baby born north of the border since 1602. The Duchess had wanted to call her second

Above: The happy family. The Duchess of York cradles Princess Margaret Rose on her knee while Princess Elizabeth embraces her mother and her father, the Duke of York.

daughter Margaret Anne, but the latter name was vetoed by the King. Lilibet instantly christened her younger sister 'Bud' explaining that she was not yet full grown.

Lady Mary recalls the young Margaret Rose well. 'She was quite unlike her sister. She was the naughty one — full of mischief, a real monkey but a charming one. She was always up to some prank. I remember once, she nearly drowned one of the royal detectives. He was bending down trying to get something out of the lake, when she leapt onto his shoulders forcing him under water. I can see her now, sitting on his shoulders laughing her head off while we all tried to pull her off.'

And so the happy, tranquil years unfolded. The Duke and Duchess acquired Royal Lodge in Windsor Great Park as their country retreat and, with the help of their daughters, created a wonderful garden. A little Welsh cottage, given to Princess Elizabeth on her sixth birthday, was built in the grounds and there were ponies and pets. The girls were frequent visitors to Glamis where they played the popular games of the day, including the rather dangerous practice of putting ha'pennies on the railway track so the oncoming train could flatten them into pennies.

On 15 January 1936, King George V, now in his seventy-first year, caught a chill while staying at Sandringham and took to his bed. The young Princesses were staying with their grandparents while their mother recovered from pneumonia and took advantage of the winter weather to make a snowman and have a snowball fight. Hearing their laughter, the King looked out of the window to watch the fun. Later that day, the princesses were on their way home after saying goodbye to Grandpapa. They were aged just nine and five. Two days later, at five minutes to midnight on 20 January, as Queen Mary

Above: Princess Margaret Rose was said to be the naughty one, but Princess Elizabeth could not resist a peek round the corner when the girls arrived with their parents at the Silver Jubilee of King George V.

Below: George V is flanked by his two sons, David, later Edward VIII, and Bertie, who became George VI.

Right: A portrait of the new Queen-Empress after the Abdication in December 1936. After the crisis was over, she wrote, 'I can hardly now believe that we have been called to this tremendous task and ... the curious thing is that we are not afraid.'

read aloud to him in the flickering firelight, King George V passed away. David was proclaimed King Edward VIII.

The Duchess of York had never liked the racy set. She hated her sister-in-law, Dorothy, married to her oldest brother, Patrick, Lord Glamis, because she smoked and drank cocktails. Therefore neither she nor Bertie, who was of the same mind, had much in common with the Fort Belvedere set who surrounded the new King and, although living close by, they were infrequent guests.

The Yorks particularly disliked the King's latest companion, Wallis Simpson, whom they had met two years before at a reception held to honour the wedding of the Duke of Kent. As her close friend Helen Hardinge recalled, 'I am afraid Mrs Simpson went down badly with the Duchess from the word go ... The

Duchess of York was never discourteous in my experience, but those of us who knew her very well could always tell when she did not care for something or someone, and it was very apparent to me that she did not care for Mrs Simpson at all.'

To make matters worse, Wallis, sensing her disapproval, took to making fun of her and dubbed her 'the Dowdy Duchess'. She was fond of mimicking her goody-goodiness which she claimed was false and artificial. On one such occasion she was caught in mid-act when the Duchess walked unexpectedly into the room. Even the young princesses' governess, Marion Crawford, did not like the look of Wallis when she visited the family at Royal Lodge. 'She was a smart, attractive woman, already middle-aged, but with that immediate friendliness American women have. She appeared to be entirely at her ease; if anything, rather too much so.'

'Chips' Channon reported that the King was 'insane' about the twice-divorced American and rumours circulated that her hold over him was due to expert sexual techniques she had learnt while on a visit to China. However, some biographers have suggested that the bout of mumps he endured during his time at Dartmouth rendered him virtually impotent, and that one of the reasons why he gave up the throne was the knowledge that he would not be able to produce an heir.

For his summer holiday in 1936 the King chartered a yacht, and Mrs Simpson and a group of friends joined him for a cruise on the Dalmatian coast. Photographs of them cavorting in the sunshine were in stark contrast to the staid family holiday of the Duke and Duchess of York in Scotland. In September the King joined them and asked if they could take on one of his public engagements, opening Aberdeen Royal Infirmary, because he was snowed under with work. They duly opened the hospital but while they were so doing the King was spotted at Ballater railway station awaiting the arrival of Mrs Simpson. As 'Chips' Channon reported, 'The visit to Balmoral was a calamity, after the King chucked opening the Aberdeen Infirmary, and then openly

THE ABDICATION CRISIS 1936

Above: Mrs Simpson in 1919 long before her romance with the King.

Left: King Edward VIII is refused a morganatic marriage to Mrs Wallis Simpson and makes the decision to abdicate.

Below: The news of the King's decision rocked the nation as people read that he could not carry the burden of kingship 'without the help and support of the woman I love.'

Left: A portrait of the Duchess of Windsor by Cecil Beaton.

HISTORIC SCENE IN COMMONS — Page 3

DAILY SKETCH

SOUVENIR NUMBER

No. 8,418   FRIDAY, DECEMBER 11, 1936   ONE PENNY

THE KING ABDICATES

PROCLAMATION OF THE DUKE

Right: The Duke of Windsor
marries Wallis Simpson on
3 June 1937 at the Château
de Candé in France.

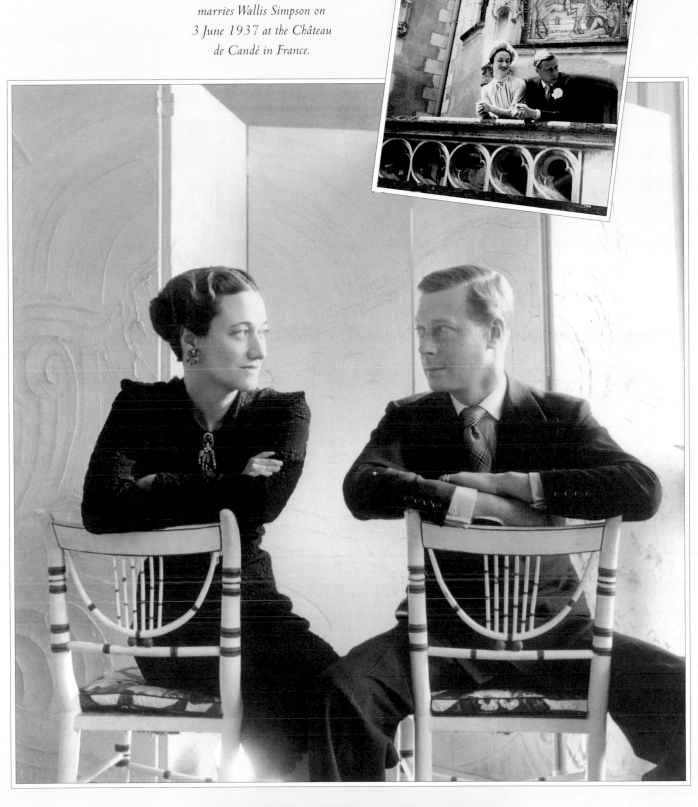

Above: The Duke and Duchess
of Windsor, in a relaxed pose,
captured by Cecil Beaton.

Left: Queen Elizabeth with
King George VI, after the
Abdication of Edward VIII
and before their Coronation on
12 May 1937. Sharing their
car, daughters Princess
Elizabeth (left) and Princess
Margaret.

appeared at Ballater station on the same day to welcome Wallis to the Highlands. Aberdeen will never forgive him.' The incident was not reported in the British press, which discreetly avoided printing any reference to Mrs Simpson.

On 27 October, Wallis received her decree nisi from Ernest Simpson and would soon be free to marry. The American press went wild and speculation was rife that she would become Edward's Queen Consort. The King knew this to be impossible and suggested a morganatic marriage, whereby any children of the union do not inherit, to the Prime Minister Stanley Baldwin. This was rejected outright by the self-governing countries of the Empire and the King announced his intention to abdicate. Shocked and hurt, Queen Mary wrote to him, 'It seemed inconceivable to those who had made such a sacrifice during the war that you, as their King, refused a lesser sacrifice. After all, all my life I have put my country before everything else, and I simply cannot change now.'

The Queen was later to describe Bertie as 'appalled' by the idea of kingship. She told her biographer Harold Nicolson, 'He was devoted to his brother and the whole abdication crisis made him miserable. He sobbed on my shoulder for a whole hour — there, upon that sofa.' In her typically understated way, she was later to describe the abdication crisis as 'a pretty kettle of fish'.

As the Duchess of York read her Bible on 10 December 1936, her husband and his younger brothers witnessed the King signing the instrument of abdication. The document was read to both houses of Parliament the next day and duly passed. That evening the departing King broadcast to the nation. He told his people that, 'I have found it impossible to carry the heavy burden of responsibility and discharge my duties as King as I would wish to do without the help and support of the woman I love.' He added that the Duke of York had 'one matchless blessing, enjoyed by so many of you and not bestowed on me, a happy home with his wife and children.' The day after her accession, the new Queen-

Empress Elizabeth was able to write, 'I can hardly now believe that we have been called to this tremendous task and ... the curious thing is that we are not afraid. I feel God has enabled us to face the situation calmly.'

Certainly one person would have been pleased, the late King George V, who had always had a fondness for Elizabeth. He had remarked of his children that 'Bertie has more guts than the rest of them put together' and in the last weeks of his life, he exclaimed passionately, after being reminded yet again of David's liaison with Wallis, 'I pray to God that my eldest son will never marry and have children, and that nothing will come between Bertie and Lilibet and the throne.' Little could he have known then that it would not be long before his wish was granted.

Above: Learning the job. Princess Margaret Rose, aged four, and Princess Elizabeth accompany their mother, the Duchess of York, on an official engagement.

71

CHAPTER THREE

QUEEN AND COUNTRY

Opposite: Cecil Beaton captures Queen Elizabeth at her most regal in this portrait taken in 1948. He was one of her favourite photographers and she posed for him many times.

Baron Charteris of Amisfield, the Queen's private secretary for twenty-seven years, has commented that the key to the Queen Mother's success was her zest for life. 'It was her totally positive attitude which helped to re-establish respect for the monarchy after the catastrophe of the abdication of her brother-in-law, King Edward VIII.'

Another former courtier goes further: 'There would have been no Royal Family today if it had not been for her,' he says. 'George VI was painfully shy and had a dreadful stammer. He desperately did not want to be King, believing he was utterly unsuited. Without Elizabeth, he would probably have gone to pieces.'

After the terrible days of the abdication crisis, Bertie was angry, tired out, astonished, bewildered, and to a certain extent, bitter. His speech impediment, which had eased so dramatically in the quiet, contented years with Elizabeth, reappeared with a vengeance. To make matters worse, the Royal Family itself was said to be split and strange stories were told about the last hours before Edward VIII finally abdicated. He was labelled 'the rubber-stamp' King, who was so weak that he would go along with whatever he was told. It was hinted that Edward VIII had really gone because he had stood up to the politicians, criticizing their lack of support for people in depressed areas, following the National Strike and the Yarrow March. Now it was suggested that the Establishment had secured themselves a 'Yes' man.

After weeks of stress, Elizabeth collapsed with an attack of flu. Queen Mary went to see her and the faithful but indiscreet governess Miss Marion Crawford, who was waiting at the door,

Above: Off duty for once, the Duke and Duchess of York relax with their daughters at their country retreat Royal Lodge, Windsor. The Duchess worried that her husband worked too hard and made his time at home as peaceful as possible.

reported, 'Queen Mary came out of the door and tears were streaming down her face. The Duchess was lying propped up among pillows. I thought that she too had been crying. She held out her hand to me. "I'm afraid there are going to be some great changes in our lives, Crawfie. We must take what is coming to us and make the best of it."'

The Prime Minister, Stanley Baldwin, had no illusions about the former King. He told the biographer Harold Nicolson: 'You see, Nicolson, the man is mad. *Mad* ... he could see nothing but that woman. He did not realize that any other considerations avail. He lacks religion ... He doesn't realize that there is anything beyond. I told his mother so.'

Mrs Keppel, his grandfather King Edward VII's mistress, commented, 'the King has shown neither decency, nor wisdom, nor regard for tradition' and his private secretary summed him up thus, 'He was without soul and this made him a trifle mad ... He never cared for England or the English ... He rather hated this country ... and did not like being reminded of his duties.'

This was to be the new Queen's finest hour. She stood four-square behind her husband and, although upset and exhausted herself, used all her courage and guile to soothe, encourage and bolster the King. She fulfilled the promise he had made on the day of his accession. 'With my wife and helpmate by my side, I take up the heavy task which lies before me.' Only her obstinate support could persuade him that he was capable and worthy of assuming the mantle of the monarchy.

Below: Down memory lane. King George VI takes his wife and daughters to visit the Royal Naval College at Dartmouth where he was a cadet before the First World War.

Opposite: *The Duke of York plays with his daughters and dogs — two corgis and a shih-tzu — outside Princess Elizabeth's playhouse which was given to her as a sixth-birthday present by the people of Wales.*

Bertie proved his gratitude on his birthday, 14 December, three days after David had left Britain, when he gave his wife the highest honour in his gift, the Order of the Garter. The Queen was touched and wrote tactfully to her mother-in-law, Queen Mary, 'He had discovered that Papa gave it to you, on his, Papa's birthday, and the coincidence was so charming that he has now followed suit and given it to me on his own birthday.' Naturally it was much more than that.

Now Bertie was settled, it was time to turn her attention to her daughters, Princess Elizabeth, aged ten, and Margaret Rose, six. There was to be an unwelcome sea change in their lives and she was determined that they would hear it from her and her alone. She had been so preoccupied and so busy in the preceding days that she initially had a discreet conference with their governess to find out what they knew. Then taking Margaret on her knee and seating Princess Elizabeth beside her, she quietly explained what had happened, the changes to come and the new responsibilities they faced. The idea of living at Buckingham Palace did not appeal to the future Queen. 'You mean for *ever?*' she asked her mother incredulously and suggested that an underground passage be dug across Green Park so she could sleep in her own bed. The Coronation of Edward VIII had been set for 12 May 1937, and after the Abdication, the Prime Minister, Stanley Baldwin, asked Parliament if it should be postponed. 'Same day. New King,' came the reply. So the Coronation was to go ahead as planned.

After a brief respite at Sandringham, when the happy news of the birth of Princess Alexandra of Kent, daughter of the Duke and Duchess of Kent, on Christmas Day lifted their spirits, Queen Elizabeth faced one of the busiest periods of her life. Not only had she and the family to move house but she had to learn the procedure of the Coronation and order her clothes for the ceremony. Her dress was made by Handley Seymour and at a long table at the Royal School of Needlework in Kensington, ten

women sat embroidering the emblems of all parts of the British Empire upon the robe. A young designer named Norman Hartnell made the dresses for her Maids of Honour. Soon he was to replace Mr Seymour as the Queen's favourite couturier.

Meanwhile the King was struggling with the monarch's red boxes, containing all the papers of State. Having never been trained in the routine duties of the sovereign, he was horrified by the amount of work that he had to get through and his meticulous eye for detail meant he spent far longer over his papers than most. Like his great-grandfather, Prince Albert, who worked himself to an early grave, he found that if things were to be done to his satisfaction, he needed to rise early and go to bed late. The Queen worried about his health and made his brief spells at home as quiet and undisturbed as possible. In addition, there was the heavy programme of official engagements, so essential to restore public confidence after the Abdication. The King and Queen picked the East End of London for their first state drive, on 13 February, and to their relief received a rousing reception at the People's Palace, a popular entertainment hall in Mile End Road. The victory of the horse Royal Mail and their presence at Aintree made the Grand National a red-letter day. At Wembley, Sunderland beat Preston North End in the FA Championship and the victorious captain received the cup and congratulations from Queen Elizabeth.

To add to the excitement, Service contingents began arriving from overseas; first the Australians, then the New Zealanders, followed by the Royal Canadian Mounted Police and hand-picked men from the regiments of India and Burma. Great electric chandeliers were hoisted into position at Westminster Abbey as the Queen took her part in rehearsals and the King worked hard with his speech therapist, Mr Logue, so that he would be word perfect on the big day.

Kings and Chiefs, Presidents and Premiers arrived daily, lions and crowns were gilded, flag poles were erected and a wide red carpet was unrolled along the Abbey's nave. The King and Queen were awoken from their sleep at three o'clock on the morning of their Coronation by a technician testing the loud speakers on Constitution Hill; the tramp of soldiers taking up their positions along the Mall coupled with the exuberant festivities of the crowds who had camped overnight made further rest impossible.

It was to be a long, triumphant and historic day. Precedent would be broken in two ways; the ceremony would be broadcast and that stickler for tradition, the Queen Dowager, Queen Mary, would overcome her prejudices and attend the crowning of her late husband's successor. Also, more than five million people would pour into the cap ital to cheer their King and Queen. The tide was beginning to turn in their favour but the royal couple were not yet home and dry.

The Princesses, despite fears that Margaret Rose might fall asleep, witnessed the ceremony, which lasted three hours and forty minutes, under the watchful eye of their grandmother, Queen Mary, and their aunt, the Princess Royal. Princess Elizabeth had asserted that it 'would be a disgrace to us all' should somnolence overtake her sis-

Above: A coronation portrait of the Royal Family. The Queen personally explained to her daughters what their new responsibilities would mean.

ter and kept her amused with books and whispered confidences.

Both King George VI and Queen Elizabeth found the cere-mony very moving. As the Duchess of Devonshire remarked, 'The Queen is a person of real piety, who felt her crowning acutely.' The Archbishop of Canterbury, Dr Lang, wrote of their spiri-tual preparation for the event. 'After some talk on the spiritual significance of the Coronation, they knelt with me; I prayed for them and for the realm and Empire, and I gave them my personal blessing. I was much moved, and so were they. Indeed, there were tears in their eyes when we rose from our knees.'

LONG LIVE OUR KING & QUEEN

Above: King George VI flanked by his mother, Queen Mary, greets the crowds from the balcony of Buckingham Palace. Princess Elizabeth, although only eleven, seems to have mastered the royal wave.

Bertie had chosen the name of George in a public attempt to emulate his father George V, who had been such a dependable and popular monarch. In his Coronation broadcast, the new King pledged, 'The Queen and I will always keep in our hearts the inspiration of this day. May we ever be worthy of the good will, which I am proud to think, surrounds us at the outset of my reign. I thank you from my heart, and may God bless you all.' However, whatever name he chose, the Prime Minister was only too aware that the new King and his Consort had a very difficult task ahead of them. There were many who felt that his older brother should not have been denied the throne for the sake of love, and a sentimental sympathy for David swept the land.

The British press, who had kept so loyally silent during much of the Wallis affair, were now in full cry. They criticized the King's poor academic record at naval college, which some even suggested made him unfit to reign. Unflattering comparisons were made between the two brothers; David was portrayed as charming and of the people. Bertie was perceived as awkward, aloof and lacking in 'presence'. His stammer was frequently mentioned as a disadvantage.

Stanley Baldwin told the faithful Mabell, Countess of Airlie, that he felt the new King was beginning his reign with a lot of prejudice against him. 'He's had no chance to capture the popular imagination as his brother did. I'm afraid he won't find it easy going for the first year or two.' Lady Airlie was more concerned for her old friend Elizabeth. 'I pitied most of all the new Queen. In the fourteen years of her marriage she had remained completely unspoiled, still at heart the simple unaffected girl I had known at Glamis, carrying out her public duties with an efficiency that won Queen Mary's admiration, but finding her true happiness in her home and her own family circle.' Queen Mary, however, was more optimistic than her lady-in-waiting. 'The Yorks will do it very well,' she confidently predicted.

And they did. In July the King and Queen visited Edinburgh and the crowds turned out to cheer them. The Queen was invested with the Order of the Thistle at St Giles Cathedral, the first lady to receive that honour. The King had surprised his Consort on the evening of his Coronation by presenting her with a beautiful diamond badge and star to be worn at her investiture.

Meanwhile the Duke of Windsor had married Wallis Simpson at the Château de Cande in France. To the former King's anger and sadness, no member of the Royal Family attended the wedding on 3 June and his wife was debarred from using the title Her

Royal Highness. The wound was never healed and was still open thirty-five years later when the Duke of Windsor died in 1972.

Society too turned its back on the Windsors and many of their friends. Despite protestations, the greatest party-giver of them all, Emerald Cunard, was never again to enjoy royal favour. Almost the only exceptions were Duff and Lady Diana Cooper, who had been frequent guests at Fort Belvedere. They were invited to Windsor Castle for the weekend and the Queen sat up late drinking tea with the diplomat. 'She put her feet up on a sofa and talked of Kingship and "the intolerable honour" but not of the crisis', he recalled. His wife commented how different was the new regime compared to the old days of Edward VIII. 'That was an operetta,' she said. 'This is an institution.' The press and the public agreed and by the end of 1937 the popularity of King George VI and his Queen was firmly established. They attracted huge crowds wherever they went and Queen Elizabeth endeared herself to the people. Ever mischievous, she once even lobbed one of her caramels through the royal car's open window to an onlooking policeman.

However, there were more troubles on the way as it became increasingly apparent that war was brewing in Europe. In March 1938, Hitler's army invaded Austria and weeks later, Czechoslovakia was at risk as the Chancellor backed a rebellion by Germans in the Sudetenland. Soon, Hitler was to announce that the country no longer existed. As the crisis intensified, it was decided that

Opposite: The look that sent fashion shock waves round the world. The Queen's white crinoline dresses and dainty parasols were admired and copied from Paris to New York. The portrait is by Cecil Beaton.

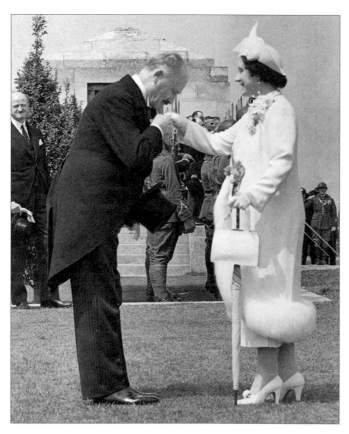

Below: Queen Elizabeth took Paris by storm when she visited France in 1938, only weeks after the death of her beloved mother, Lady Strathmore.

Above: Like her mother, Queen Elizabeth valued family life and created a happy and secure environment for her husband and daughters. Teatime was especially important when the family gathered round the fire at Buckingham Palace to talk over the events of the day.

Opposite: A rare moment of peace. The Queen relaxes with Princess Margaret Rose (left) and Princess Elizabeth in the sun-drenched gardens of Royal Lodge, Windsor.

Below: The Queen plays with one of the corgis. From earliest childhood, she always loved dogs.

Above: The King and Queen join in the singing at the annual boy's camp at Abergeldy Castle near Balmoral. Within two weeks Britain was at war and these same young men were joining up to fight for their country.

the King and Queen should visit the allies – France, Canada and the United States.

Shortly before the first of these visits, the Queen's mother, Lady Strathmore, died at the age of seventy-five. The tour was postponed for three weeks but then her daughter, valiant as ever, 'captured Paris by storm' in her white mourning dresses – a *tour de force* by designer Sir Norman Hartnell. In Canada, the royal couple were welcomed by crowds estimated at over half a million and in Washington they received a tumultuous reception. One Texan member of the House of Representatives declared, 'Cousin

Elizabeth, you're a thousand times more pretty than your pictures.'

Their duty very well done, the family travelled to Balmoral in August where the King held his annual boys' camp at Abergeldy Castle, a few miles away. As the Royal Family joined in a sing-song, Hitler was preparing to invade Poland. The King returned to London with the Queen close on his heels. Within two weeks. Britain was at war and the young men of the King's camp were joining the services. It was said the Queen was 'a tower of strength' and she in turn took strength from her faith, recalling the Bowes Lyon family motto 'In thou, my God, I place my trust without changes to the end.' It had seen her through difficult times before and would do so again.

At Buckingham Palace, staff immediately rejoined their regiments and a Home Guard was formed among those who remained. It was decided that the Princesses should be evacuated to Windsor but the King and Queen steadfastly refused to leave London, even during the Blitz. As the 'few' fought over the skies in the Battle of Britain in 1940 and invasion seemed imminent, it was suggested that Elizabeth and Margaret Rose be sent to Canada but the Queen was having none of it. 'The Princesses will never leave without me. I will not leave without the King — and the King will never leave,' she asserted. During the worst of the bombing, they visited the East End of London to witness for themselves the carnage and destruction. As one of the women wrote to Dame Barbara Cartland, herself very

Below: Wartime precautions in case of fire at Buckingham Palace.

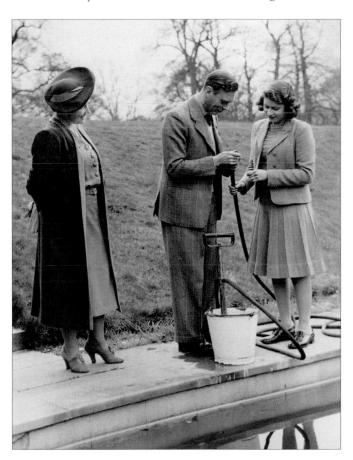

THE SECOND WORLD WAR

Right: King George VI speaks to the nation on the outbreak of war on 3 September 1939. A gallant veteran of the Battle of Jutland, he was only too aware of the dangers Britain faced and the sacrifice that would be needed to avert Nazi invasion.

IN THE NEWS · **Blast Toll at 35; Probes On** · 7TH SPORT WALL ST. CLOSING

Journal American · LARGEST EVENING CIRCULATION IN AMERICA ·

KING, QUEEN SAFE IN PALACE BOMBING

Sealise Case Goes to Jury · **Blast Origin Baffles Inquiry**

Kelly Tells How He'll Toughen U.S. · **Japs Mass Ships Off Indo-China** · **3 More Attacks Hammer London** · **Raider Hits Downing St.**

Left and above: The King and Queen view the bomb damage in the quadrangle at Buckingham Palace. Their London home was hit a total of nine times and, on one occasion, they only escaped being injured by diving under a table. However, they refused to leave London during the Blitz.

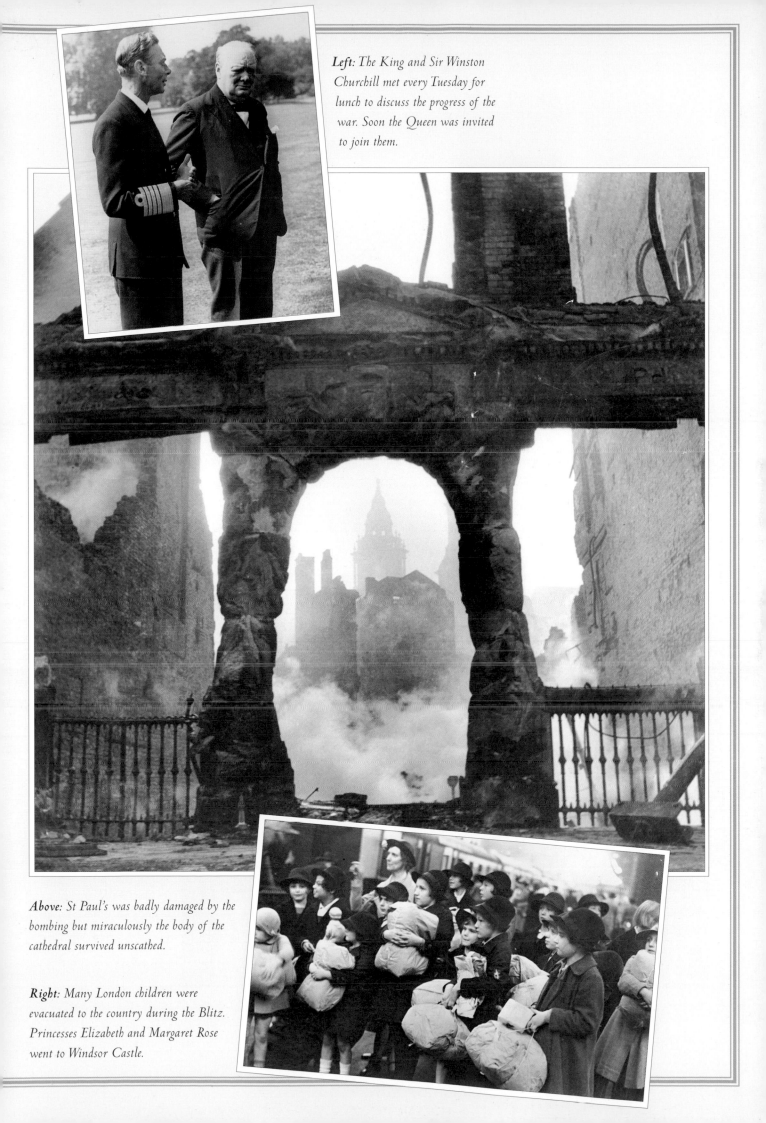

Left: The King and Sir Winston Churchill met every Tuesday for lunch to discuss the progress of the war. Soon the Queen was invited to join them.

Above: St Paul's was badly damaged by the bombing but miraculously the body of the cathedral survived unscathed.

Right: Many London children were evacuated to the country during the Blitz. Princesses Elizabeth and Margaret Rose went to Windsor Castle.

active during the war, 'The Queen came down yesterday morning – God bless her. She was so kind and she said to me: "I am so sorry for you. I know what you are feeling." The way she spoke was like the voice of an angel. Though I hadn't shed a tear over my home in ruins, and my little dog dead, I cried like a baby. There's never been a lady like her – and that's the truth.'

The Queen wrote to her mother-in-law, Queen Mary, 'I feel quite exhausted after seeing and hearing so much sadness, sorrow, heroism and magnificent spirit. The destruction is so awful and the people are so wonderful – they deserve a better world.' When Buckingham Palace was hit, she remarked, 'I'm glad we've been bombed. It makes me feel I can look the East End in the face.' The Palace was bombed nine times in all and the Guards Chapel, nearby, was completely destroyed killing over 100 worshippers.

Mr Chris Friend, Pearly King of the Isle of Dogs and Poplar,

Below: The King and Queen visiting a bomb shelter during the Blitz.

remembers her visit well. 'I was about thirteen at the time and it is a day I will never forget. The streets were full of rubble. People were living in terrible conditions. Families were living on the pavement or in the basements of the bombed-out buildings. As she picked her way through the destruction, she had a word for everybody. People couldn't believe it. She just came and chatted as if she had known them all her life. She was in the same predicament and it was a real morale booster to the whole of the East End. My mother and her friends were in tears, something I had never seen before and was never to see again. She was fabulous. We never forgot her and she never forgot us. As far as we

Above: Queen Elizabeth comforts the homeless in Stepney. 'I'm glad we've been bombed,' she declared after the Palace was hit. 'It makes me feel I can look the East End in the face.'

91

Above, opposite and below: *The King and Queen, sometimes with Princess Elizabeth at their side, were tireless in visiting every corner of Britain promoting the war effort. In her spare time, the Queen made bandages for the Red Cross while the King spent two evenings a week making ammunition.*

were concerned she was the greatest royal favourite there has ever been, and she would always be Number One.' And the people of the East End were as good as their word. Every year, on her birthday, a huge cake was delivered with the compliments of those she comforted through the bad times they all endured.

It was to be the same throughout Britain. The King and Queen travelled the length and breadth of the nation on the royal train giving sympathy and support. Hardly a battle station, factory or farm was ignored as they comforted the homeless and bereaved and spurred on the troops. It might have been Churchill's finest hour but it was theirs too. While the former King had visited Berlin just before the war and allied himself with the Fascists, the British people rejected Nazism in all its seductive guises and with it, David, Edward VIII. Despite many requests to be involved and allowed to return to the country in a time of crisis, the Duke was kept safely out of the way as Governor of the Bahamas.

On 25 August 1942, the Duke of Kent left Balmoral Castle, after spending a few days with the King and Queen, to fly to Iceland where he was due to inspect RAF bases. But his plane crashed in the Scottish mountains and he was killed. The King, who had been very close to his younger brother, was devastated. A year earlier, the Queen's nephew, John, Lord Glamis, had been killed in

action. The Royal Family not only shared the personal bereavement of their people but also the privations of war. As the American President's wife, Eleanor Roosevelt, noted when she visited in 1942, rationing was as strict at the Palace as it was elsewhere. 'We were served on gold and silver plates, but our bread was the same kind of war bread every other family had to eat ... nothing was ever served that was not served in any war canteen.'

Green lines were painted on baths to ensure that no one was tempted to use too much hot water; the magnificent gardens at Royal Lodge were dug up and turned over to vegetables, tended by the Princesses; and shooting ranges were constructed both at Buckingham Palace and Windsor. Every morning the Queen received instruction in how to fire a revolver, declaring, 'I shall not go down like the others.' To help, Churchill sent her an automatic weapon of great efficiency.

The Royal Family were also anxious to make sure that they contributed to the war effort in a personal way. The Queen and her staff made bandages and dressings for the Red Cross, while the King spent two evenings a week making ammunition. Princess Elizabeth was also keen to do her bit and plagued her father to be allowed to join one of the women's services as soon as she passed her sixteenth birthday. The King thought her too young but was finally persuaded by the Queen and in March 1945, she entered the records of the Auxiliary Territorial Service as No. 230873 Second Subaltern

Below: Princess Elizabeth enlisted in the Auxiliary Territorial Service and learnt how to drive and to change lorry wheels. 'Last night we had sparking plugs during the whole of dinner!' joked her mother.

Elizabeth Alexandra Mary Windsor. The princess learnt how to drive and to change the wheels on a lorry and as the Queen told one of her senior officers, 'Last night we had sparking plugs during the whole of dinner!'

Although the Queen was strict as far as her daughters' education was concerned, she also made sure that they had their fair share of fun. She arranged birthday parties and dances at Windsor Castle and invited young Guards officers, stationed at depots nearby. These were highly informal affairs of the 'knees up' variety with games and music after supper. It became routine for the King and Queen to lead congas round the ballroom.

Meanwhile, in Princess Elizabeth's room was a photograph of a handsome young naval officer. Letters were passing between Prince Philip and herself, and during his leaves they met on a number of occasions. They danced at a party given by the Duchess of Kent and, at Christmas 1943, he was among the guests invited to Windsor. As usual there was the annual pantomime; Elizabeth played Aladdin and Margaret Rose, the Princess. Elizabeth is said to have given a particularly sparkling performance as the young Lieutenant watched from the front row. 'Philip thinks this' and 'Philip thinks that' began to pepper her daily conversation.

On 8 May 1945, the unconditional surrender of Germany was announced and the war was over in Europe. The crowds surged up the Mall to cheer the King and Queen, flanked by their daughters and Sir Winston Churchill, as they stood on the balcony of Buckingham Palace. Amid scenes of wild jubilation, the VE Day celebrations continued far into the night and the Princesses asked if they might join the revellers. 'Poor darlings,' said the King, 'they've never had any fun yet' and permission was given on condition that they were escorted by a small party of male friends.

The girls slipped out of a side entrance and, unrecognized, joined the throng as they cheered their parents. Then, going with

Above: Victory at last. The King and Queen flank Prime Minister Sir Winston Churchill on the balcony of Buckingham Palace to acknowledge the cheers of the crowd. Meanwhile the young Princesses were doing the conga through all the best hotels in town.

the tide of the crowd, they were swept along the Mall and Whitehall before ending up doing the conga through all the best hotels in town. During their two-hour foray, Princess Margaret stole a sailor's hat and the unfortunate man chased her all the way back to the Palace, never realizing who she was. Our present Queen was to say of the outing, 'I think it was one of the most memorable moments of my life.'

It was said of Lady Strathmore that she had 'a genius for family life' and it was a trait her youngest daughter inherited. Teatime became a vocal point in the life of the Royal Family when they all gathered together round the fire to discuss the events of the day and any problems that had arisen. One topic that came up increasingly frequently was Princess Elizabeth's cousin, Lieutenant Philip Mountbatten. The pair had fallen in love during the war years and now wished to announce their engagement at Christmas 1946. However, the King and Queen thought otherwise, and wished there to be a pause to make sure the couple were certain of their feelings. So both Princesses joined their parents on a four-month tour of South Africa in the New Year of 1947, with a certain Group Captain Peter Townsend going as their equerry. While Princess Elizabeth pined for her sweetheart, a friendship between her younger sister, Princess Margaret Rose, then sixteen, and the Group Captain began. Little did they know it was to cause them both heartache.

Below: Princess Elizabeth, in stockinged feet, walks through the South African bush after sacrificing her footwear to her mother during the royal tour of 1947. The Queen had earlier lost a heel. Group Captain Peter Townsend can be seen in the background second from right.

Below: The smiles say it all. The King had made them wait a year to be sure of their feelings but now, at last, Princess Elizabeth and Prince Philip announce their engagement on 9 July 1947. The Princess showed off her diamond and platinum ring at a Palace garden party.

On 9 July, Princess Elizabeth and Prince Philip announced their engagement and the Princess proudly showed off her platinum and diamond ring at the garden party that afternoon. The marriage took place at Westminster Abbey on 20 November, the first great State occasion since the war and the huge crowds were determined to enjoy themselves despite the times of austerity. The King wrote to his newly married daughter, 'I was so proud of you and thrilled at having you so close to me on our long walk in Westminster Abbey, but when I handed your hand to the Archbishop I felt I had lost something very precious.'

Princess Margaret, however, was still at home and was the apple of the King's eye. 'He adored both his daughters,' recalls a courtier, 'but Margaret, he spoilt.' With her quick wit, she could make him laugh even when he was angry with her and she got away with murder. Once, when she was asked by her parents not to be so free with the sherry bottle, she replied firmly that she would launch no more ships unless her glass was refilled. When she was questioned about her use of modern slang, she joked that she had learnt it, 'At my mother's knee, or some such low joint.'

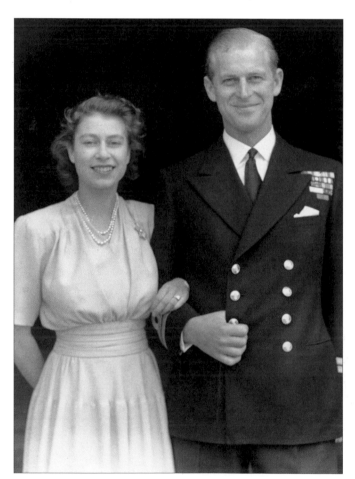

She was 'Papa's girl' and they delighted in each other's company. When he was not very well or feeling rather low, she would sing funny songs to amuse him and would mimic mutual friends. Charades was another favourite entertainment and it was not unknown for the King to don a false moustache and a cardboard policeman's helmet from a cracker to add to the fun. But soon there were to be fewer parties as the King's health deteriorated. When Prince Charles was born on 14 November 1948, his grandfather was lying ill under the same roof. Doctors were called to investigate cramp in his legs and they discovered hardening of the arteries which later necessitated an operation. The Queen and Princess Elizabeth took on an increasing load of official duties as the King was ordered to rest. Shortly after the birth of Princess Anne on 15 August 1950, he was found to have cancer and had to have a lung removed. Princess Elizabeth rang every day from Canada, fearing she might never see her father again.

In December 1951, the King was well enough to pre-record his Christmas broadcast and went, as usual, to Sandringham for the New Year. He told his family that he felt so much better that

Above: The wedding took place at Westminster Abbey on 20 November, the first great State occasion since the war. The public loved every minute of the celebrations but the King confessed, 'I felt I had lost something very precious.'

Above: King George VI's last illness. The King shows the ravages of cancer after the duties of monarchy and the strain of winning a 'bloody' war take their toll.

he was happy to send Princess Elizabeth and the Duke of Edinburgh away on a five-month tour of Australia and New Zealand, visiting Kenya on the way. On the eve of their departure, the whole family spent an evening at the Theatre Royal, Drury Lane, enjoying the première of the musical *South Pacific*. Despite the bitter cold of a late January day, the King stood bareheaded on the tarmac to wave his daughter goodbye, not returning into the warmth of the Heathrow terminal until the last speck of her aeroplane had disappeared. A week later, on 6 February, the King died in his sleep, aged fifty-six, at Sandringham after enjoying a good day's shooting.

The new Queen heard the news after spending the night in a tree-house in Kenya watching big game. She returned immediately to London, wearing the black mourning clothes packed in her travelling wardrobes — just in case. As the light was fading, she stepped on to British soil, and a letter was handed to her in her mother's hand. 'Her old Grannie and subject must be the first to kiss her hand.' At half past four Queen Mary drove from Marlborough House to Clarence House to pay obedience to the new monarch, the seventh she had known. Queen Elizabeth, the new Queen Mother, faced widowhood at the age of fifty-one.

The Duke and Duchess of Windsor had received the news of the King's death by telephone in their six-room apartment on the twenty-eighth floor of the Waldorf Towers in New York. On the evening of the following day, the Windsors held a press

Opposite: A very special kind of closeness. Many presumed that the King had relied on his extrovert wife, but when he died, they realized how much she had depended on him. When praised for her many acheivements, Queen Elizabeth always said, 'It was not me. It was us together.'

conference in the Verandah Grill on the sun deck of the Cunard liner, *Queen Mary*, surrounded by gum-chewing reporters, photographers and cameramen. Around them were impressionistic decorations of acrobats, ballet dancers, a witch and her cauldron, and a cat. It was, as one observer commented, 'the most macabre setting in which British royalty can ever have appeared.' The Duke journeyed back to London alone – neither the widowed Queen nor David and Bertie's mother, Queen Mary, were prepared to tolerate the presence of Wallis. Weeks after the funeral, the Queen Mother was to refer to her as, 'the woman who killed my husband.'

The late King, described in the *Daily Mirror* as 'by any standards, anywhere, a good man', lay in State in Westminster Hall. His mother, sister and older brother went to pay their respects. The Duke of Windsor dropped on one knee as he entered and left the Hall, but otherwise showed no emotion. Bertie was buried in St George's Chapel, Windsor, awash with flowers from the famous to the unknown. Fulham street traders sent their tokens of respect as did Churchill – in his case a wreath in the shape of the George Cross which bore the words at its centre, 'For Gallantry'. The Queen Mother's tribute of white orchids, lilies and carnations, said simply, 'For my darling Bertie, from his always loving Elizabeth.'

While many had perceived the Queen Mother as being stronger than her husband, it now became evident that this was far from the truth. Lady Cynthia Colville, long-time friend and Woman of the Bedchamber to Queen Mary wrote, 'Few people

Opposite: King George VI's funeral. As the Daily Mirror *put it, he was 'by any standards, anywhere, a good man' and the nation rose to honour him in an avalanche of flowers. Churchill sent a wreath in the shape of the George Cross which bore the words at its centre, 'For Gallantry'. Wallis was banned from the ceremony and the Duke of Windsor came alone.*

realized how much she had relied on *him* – on his capacity for wise and detached judgement, for sound advice, and how lost she now felt without him.' As the Queen Mother was to say, when praised by admirers for her accomplishments, 'It was not me, it was us together.'

There were now fears that the Queen Mother would retreat from public life to the northernmost tip of Scotland where, in the first weeks of her widowhood, she had bought the derelict Castle of Mey. However, Sir Winston Churchill persuaded her that her duty remained with her family and the nation. While many years earlier, she would have distrusted his judgement, the Second World War had bonded a close friendship and she now felt inspired by his words. Her daughter, the new Queen, sent her a red leather dispatch box embossed in gold with 'HM Queen Elizabeth, the Queen Mother', and ensured that she was eligible to serve as a Counsellor of State during the Sovereign's absence. The message was clear.

Only three months after the King's death, the Queen Mother fulfilled her first public engagement, saying farewell to her own regiment and that of her brothers, the Black Watch, as they left to fight in Korea. A few weeks later she surprised the territorials of the regiment when they came across her, at five o'clock in the morning, during a route march. Backs were suddenly straightened and shoulders squared as they spotted through the mist above Balmoral Castle their Colonel-in-Chief, complete with corgi, wrapped in a thick woolly overcoat and old felt hat. She was back on duty and in character. As Bertie would have wished, she was soldiering on.

Her father's death also left a terrible gap for Princess Margaret. 'Life seemed to stand still when Papa died. I cannot believe that I will grow old without seeing him again.' Now sleep was difficult and her appetite, always slight, was next to nothing. This had been her first real encounter with death and in her lonely suite at the opposite end of the Palace to that of her mother, who was also totally isolated in her grief, Margaret felt the full pain of the parting. Her calm and supportive older sister was absent, preoccupied with taking on the affairs of State and her own young family. So she turned increasingly for comfort and friendship to the Queen Mother's new Comptroller, Peter Townsend. Newly divorced, he found in the young Princess a sympathetic ear for his troubles and within a year, had confessed that he was in love with her. 'That is exactly how I feel, too,' she admitted.

The couple were discreet, talking while walking on the hill or riding together in Windsor Great Park, but the tiniest of gestures after the new Queen's Coronation was to make their romance public. As they waited in Westminster Great Hall, a radiant Princess cut through the throng and, like a wife, brushed a small speck of fluff from his uniform. The body language was obvious — they were in love, and the world now knew it.

Princess Elizabeth, now the new Queen, had known for some considerable time how her sister felt about Group Captain Townsend. While she bottled up the terrible premature loss of her father, she had to confront the first crisis of her reign. For once her mother, who was grieving the loss of her husband, was of no help. She had her own problems and the decision was up to others. As one courtier recalled, 'Queen Elizabeth did not see what she did not want to see. She left it to others to deal with the situation. Matters were now out of her hands.'

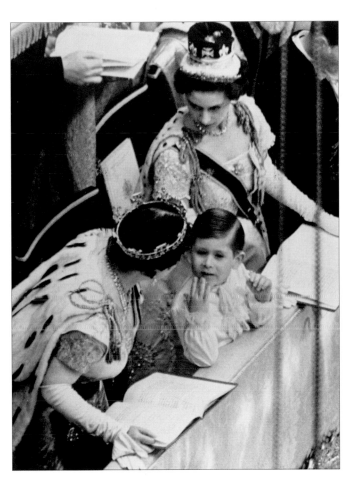

Above: Four-year-old Prince Charles turns to his beloved Grannie during the Coronation of his mother, the Queen, as Princess Margaret lends a helping hand. Queen Elizabeth, the Queen Mother, was to be 'both mother and father to him' as her daughter took on the heavy burdens of State.

As Defender of the Faith and temporal Governor of the Church of England, the Queen, according to a close courtier, 'Hid her head in the red boxes.' She did not want to hurt her sister. But, weighed against this were the duties and responsibilities that she had learnt from her grandmother, Queen Mary, and from her father. She was determined, she said, 'that she would *never* let him down.' Meanwhile her sister was saying bitterly, 'You look after the Empire and I will look after my life.' In her distress and perhaps out of spite, Margaret suggested to her sister that she might care to take a closer look at Prince Philip's 'private' social engagements. The thought was to lurk in the Queen's mind for some time.

As a senior courtier later said, 'The Queen simply could not bear it. She buried herself in her work and hoped the situation would go away. She loved her sister but everyone was telling her that any marriage was impossible.' Shrewd as ever, the Queen Mother eventually came up with a solution – a 1,500-mile tour to Rhodesia, now Zimbabwe. Meanwhile, Townsend was dispatched to Brussels. For two years the Princess and Group Captain Townsend were kept apart and did not meet.

In August 1955, Princess Margaret turned twenty-five and was free to marry without royal consent. However, the terms of such a union were onerous. Not only would she lose her rank and her £6,000 a year allowance but she would probably have to live abroad for a while. It was generally considered that marriage to Townsend would weaken the link with Commonwealth countries and that, at home, it would create a difficult position between the Crown, the Church and the Government. The Queen Mother was definitely against the match and she was more rigid in her attitude than the Queen. She had been trained by Queen Mary, and just as her mother-in-law had put duty before love at the time of the Abdication, so did the Queen Mother now. 'Would her father King George VI have approved of such a marriage?' she asked Princess Margaret. The answer was clearly not. The Queen

Left: The Queen Mother with Lord Snowdon and Princess Margaret shortly after their engagement. Although the marriage ended in divorce, Queen Elizabeth was on the best of terms with the famous photographer and doted on their children.

Mother had seen her husband die because of the value he placed on duty, now she could point out to her youngest daughter where her duty lay.

'She was immensely understanding during the Townsend affair,' says a former aide. 'She has always had sympathy. She is not one to go rushing into angry speeches. She will listen and sympathize and not dictate at all. She will just try to quietly lead whoever is in trouble on to the right path. It is significant that when Princess Margaret announced that she would not marry Peter Townsend, she did so from under Clarence House's roof.' As Princess Margaret was ruefully to remark, 'When you're royal, not even your love is your own.' This comment from the young Princess was to prove particularly poignant in her own life.

CHAPTER FOUR

SPECIAL RELATIONSHIPS

Opposite and below:
Banks of flowers pile
up outside Buckingham
Palace as Britain
grieves for Diana,
Princess of Wales.
Her death changed the
face of the monarchy
for ever.

The shocking death of Diana, Princess of Wales, on the last day of August 1997, plunged the Royal Family into the greatest crisis it had experienced for over sixty years. Not since the Abdication of King Edward VIII in 1936 had the throne rocked more precariously as the public turned its face against the monarchy in the days of hysterical grieving that followed the tragic Paris car crash. For the first time in her reign, the Queen felt a cold shiver of unpopularity as the entrenched traditions of the Palace proved too inflexible to respond to the mood of the nation. The Royal Family was perceived as uncaring as its members hid their personal feelings behind a well-worn mask of majesty while others, including Prime Minister Tony Blair, spoke in emotional terms about 'The People's Princess'. This was a catch-phrase that would come to embody the Princess's life and a mantle that the monarch, albeit belatedly, would try to take on.

One of the most potent symbols of the gulf between the Queen and her subjects, and one that enraged even her most loyal supporters, was the absence of a flag flying at half-mast above

Buckingham Palace. As official buildings throughout Britain demonstrated this mark of respect for Diana, courtiers explained in vain that protocol dictated that the royal standard could not follow suit. At a time of national mourning, when the public looked to her for leadership and mutual support, the Queen was absent, on holiday and out of sight behind the walls of her Scottish castle, Balmoral. To the tearful crowds surging up the Mall, clutching the flowers that they were to lay at the gates of

Right: The Queen Mother was the first member of the Royal Family to communicate with the people at ease. As Duchess of York, she visited Abereyon Colliery and discussed the finer points of a miner's lamp.

her London residence, it was incomprehensible that the Queen they had so long respected appeared to care so little for the Princess they loved.

The lessons of that time have been well learnt. Gone are the days when One was surrounded by One's pals and a discreet word in an editor's ear would still stop press attention. Increasingly, the royal 'firm' is becoming like any other Department of State, complete with spin doctors, special advisers and highly paid press officers. The modern ways and means of Government now prevail in the red plush corridors behind the Palace's formal Victorian façade.

How different might it have been if that other 'commoner', Queen Elizabeth, the Queen Mother, also an earl's daughter and not a princess of the blood royal, had stood in her eldest daughter's shoes during that troubled time. A forerunner of Diana, it was she who first brought a breath of fresh air into the stuffy formality of the court of King George V. It was she who pioneered the first walkabout and it was she who first spoke to people in language that they could understand. Indeed, according to Dame

Above: Waterloo station — up on his toes goes Prince Charles, just days after his sixth birthday, with a huge hug for Grannie. Princess Anne, four, patiently waits her turn.

Barbara Cartland, she once addressed a man earnestly about his bicycle – to his utter astonishment. Such a down-to-earth attitude allied to her charismatic charm, might have meant that she sidestepped the pitfalls into which the unfortunate Queen so innocently and unknowingly fell.

However, the Queen, despite her many gifts and undoubted qualities, cannot be like her mother. While the Queen Mother was a natural extrovert, who announced as a very young child that her hobby was 'liking people', the Queen found it difficult to show her feelings and retreated behind a distant formality, which made her appear cold. Never was this better illustrated than when she and Prince Philip returned from a long foreign tour and were met at the station by six-year-old Prince Charles and four-year-old Princess Anne. Mother and son exchanged a handshake but from Grannie there was a huge hug. As a former courtier explains, 'She [the Queen] had been trained like a trooper never to show her feelings and she is by nature a fairly undemonstrative person. She was a good parent in that she was absolutely fair and very consistent. The children always knew exactly where they stood with her and she was very firm. But she failed as a parent because she was unable to show

Below: Waterloo station again. The Queen finally returns home from a lengthy Commonwealth tour. She never found it easy to show affection in public.

emotion. She never found it easy to hug her children; in fact, she wasn't a woman for hugging at all. She never indulged them in any way and as for crying – that was definitely out.'

It was a very different story when Prince Charles and Princess Anne went to see their grandparents. In the words of a close friend, King George VI and Queen Elizabeth 'spoilt them to death. In their eyes they could do no wrong. Prince Charles was the apple of the King's eye – the longed-for son he had never had.' Godfrey Talbot, the BBC's Court Correspondent from 1948 to 1969, asserts that 'it was generally believed that Prince Charles was better for Grandpapa's health than any amount of medicine'.

When the Queen went to Malta for a holiday with her husband, then an officer in the Royal Navy, Charles and Anne were left behind with their grandparents. During their stay, their grandfather wrote to his daughter: 'Charles is too sweet, stumping about the room. We shall love having him at Sandringham. He is the fifth generation to live there and I hope he will get to love the place.' Christmas brought two white tricycles, presents from their parents, which despite the weather, the children could not wait to try out. 'They were riding through the large state rooms of Sandringham House, ringing their bells and shouting "Fire, fire" at the tops of their voices. Queen Elizabeth asked them to stop and come and meet the guests,' recalls a courtier. '"Oh no, we can't do that Grannie," said Prince Charles, "There's a fire you see and we have *got* to put it out." Far from being cross, Queen Elizabeth just laughed.'

On another occasion, Princess Anne begged to be allowed to go to church with the rest of the family. Her request was naturally indulged but she was warned that she must behave absolutely perfectly. 'All

Opposite and below: Devoted grandparents at Prince Charles's third birthday party. The Queen Mother holds fifteen-month old Princess Anne, while King George VI, recovering from an operation to remove a lung, is about to have a man-to-man chat with his grandson. He died of cancer eleven weeks later.

Right: Princess
Elizabeth plays with
Prince Charles at
Clarence House. Soon
the carefree days would
be over and she would
be Queen.

went well until the congregation was solemnly kneeling to say the prayer for the Royal Family,' remembers a fellow guest. 'As we were all calling on God to bless and protect Philip, Duke of Edinburgh, Charles, Prince of Wales, and other members of the Royal Family, Princess Anne, much to her brother's embarrassment, leapt to her feet and yelled at the top of her voice, "Duke of Cornflakes" before bursting out laughing. Naturally, she was hustled out of church but we were all quite surprised that she didn't really get into trouble.' Prince Philip, however, was not amused. 'He used to complain to his wife that her parents were much too soft with the children and they were getting out of hand.'

The King's death brought Prince Charles and the Queen Mother even closer together. 'From the moment the King died, the Queen didn't have a minute to spare. She was plunged straight in at the deep end and immediately had to take over all the responsibilities of State,' recalls Mr Talbot. 'She had been trained since the cradle by her father that duty came before everything, including family. She reluctantly had to abandon her children and they virtually didn't see their parents for months on end. It was very upsetting and bewildering for the little boy, and he turned to Grannie for a shoulder to cry on. During the first years of the

Below: The new Queen comes home after her father's sudden death.

Queen's reign, the Queen Mother was both mother and father to them. In the full family sense, she took over domestically.'

Although two years younger, Princess Anne's attitude to her grandmother was more robust and she seemed to take the changes in her stride. Always the tomboy, she seemed the older of the pair and was the first to climb trees, ride ponies and whizz round on scooters. As their nanny, Mabel Anderson, remembers, 'He was never as boisterous or noisy as Princess Anne. She had a much stronger, more extrovert personality. She didn't exactly push him aside, but she was certainly a more forceful child. She was better with her hands, while Charles was all fingers and thumbs. She was always the ringleader and up to every sort of prank you can think of. Charles just tagged along.' A family friend recalls that when they were each given a pair of boxing gloves Prince Philip had to confiscate them because Charles 'seemed to be getting the worst of it.'

The young Prince and Princess loved staying with the Queen Mother in the informal atmosphere of Clarence House or Birkhall in Scotland. 'Her door was always open. She loved them joining her in the drawing-room for tea round the fire and then playing games,' says Mr Talbot. 'She made everything very cosy and homely which was just what they needed.' It was the Queen Mother who first awakened in Charles a love of music. 'She used to take him to the odd concert as a treat and he would sit there mesmerized. It was the outing that he particularly looked forward to,' he adds. The pair would also spend long days on the River Dee where the Queen Mother introduced him to her favourite sport, fishing. Even today, her grandson will travel as far as Iceland in the hope of landing a large salmon.

Of Prince Charles the Queen Mother once said: 'He is a very gentle boy, with a very kind heart, which I think is the essence of everything.' And he has described Grannie: 'Ever since I can remember, my grandmother has been the most wonderful example of fun, laughter, warmth, infinite security and, above all else,

Above: Prince Charles loved his sister Princess Anne, shown here at her christening, and was always very protective towards her. It was Andrew he 'really fought with'.

exquisite taste in so many things.' But life at home was very different.

As a friend of the Royal Family noted. 'Like many other aristocratic families, the Queen and Prince Philip chose to bring up their children in the traditional way. Offspring were definitely to be seen and not heard and the youngsters were firmly in the charge of Nanny. The children might see their parents at breakfast time or perhaps be summoned to the drawing-room for tea but like many others their daily lives were behind the green baize door. It was in many ways a typical Victorian upbringing. Mummy was a remote and glamorous figure who came to kiss you goodnight, smelling of lavender and dressed for dinner. Prince Charles worshipped his mother, the Queen – but from afar.'

To make matters worse, while Princess Anne's high spirits endeared her to her father, Prince Philip's relationship with his son was never good. 'He was the antithesis of his thrusting, sure-of-himself father and sometimes a disappointment to him. While he respected him, he was also in awe of him. The Duke's near-Teutonic orders and demands frightened him and made him more reticent,' recalls a courtier. 'It was really a vicious circle. The more exasperated the Duke became, the more he [Charles] went back into his shell.' His governess, Catherine Peebles – nicknamed Mispy (for Miss P) – noticed the same tendency. 'He liked being amused rather than amusing himself. He was very responsive to kindness, but if you shouted at him, he would draw back into his shell for a time and you could do nothing with him.' The Queen tried to intervene in the friction between father and son but it was really no good. 'They were just incompatible,' says a courtier.

Opposite: The Queen Mother took over domestically when her daughter became Sovereign. Princess Anne and Prince Charles were never happier.

However, the Queen Mother took a somewhat less rosy view of the Earl. As the Queen once told a friend, 'Mummy has never forgiven Dickie for introducing David [King Edward VIII] to Wallis Simpson. She has always felt that the burden of being King was responsible for my father's early death.' Lord Mountbatten's late private secretary, John Barratt, went further: 'On account of his association with David, I believe the Queen Mother was always wary of him. They greeted each other cordially, and before his death she even visited Broadlands, but they were never comfortable together. I believe that, even in her old age, Queen Elizabeth felt betrayed by the Duke of Windsor, who so summarily propelled her ill-prepared husband to the throne. She was also aware that she and Bertie, before he became King, were never part of the glamorous set in which David and the Mountbattens moved, and I think she always felt a resentment towards them.'

When Lord Mountbatten's wife, Edwina, died and, at her own wish, was buried at sea, the Queen Mother remarked acidly, 'Poor Edwina, she always did like to make a splash.' But there was more to it than this. A senior courtier explains that the Queen Mother 'was very suspicious of Lord Mountbatten's motives. He had successfully engineered the marriage between the Queen and his nephew, Prince Philip. Now he was turning his attentions to finding a suitable bride for Prince Charles and was pushing the cause of his granddaughter, Amanda Knatchbull, very hard. He very much wanted her to be the next Princess of Wales.'

The Earl had laid his plans well. When Prince Charles brought his latest girlfriend Camilla, later Parker-Bowles, to stay at Broadlands, his 'honorary grandfather' was emphatic. 'Have fun with her by all means,' he counselled, 'but for God's sake don't get involved. She's far too common. You could never marry her. The country wouldn't have it.' The lovelorn Prince dithered and went off to Canada to consider these weighty words. By the time he came home, Camilla had got fed up with hanging around waiting for him to make up his mind and had married someone else.

'He was heartbroken but it was too late,' remembers a courtier.

The way was now clear for the Earl to pursue his dynastic ambitions. If he was to turn a childhood friendship into a romance, Lord Mountbatten was well aware that the inexperienced Amanda, with her ethnic off-the-peg clothes, would have to be transformed into the type of polished, sophisticated lady that the Prince found attractive. In great secrecy – for her parents, Lord and Lady Brabourne, would have been furious if they had known what he was scheming – he sent her off to Paris to buy designer outfits and get her hair done – and he then despatched the pair to the Bahamian island of Eleuthera. Prince Charles dutifully proposed but Amanda only laughed and said, 'What a funny idea'.

According to John Barratt, 'Lord Mountbatten began to get tough with the Prince'. He bombarded Charles with letters, pointing out 'that no girl, not just Amanda, would be thrilled at the prospect of becoming Princess of Wales. It was asking them to give up a lot, and the rewards would not necessarily compensate for the loss of privacy.' Charles was surprised at this and promised to try harder.

In 1979, three months before he was assassinated by the IRA, the Earl was picking out presents for Charles to give Amanda and was planning for them to meet during Prince Charles's tour of India. He would naturally be there to push things along. 'It was going to be Lord Mountbatten's ace hand: he thought that if he could get the two of them together, relaxed and away from pressures, for at least some of the time, they would be drawn even closer. He was quite confident that the magic of India would do the trick,' reports his private secretary.

None of these machinations was lost on the Queen Mother and her distrust and dislike for the Earl gradually increased. 'They met very rarely,' says a senior courtier 'but when they did, they were very cautious of each other. They circled each other like the

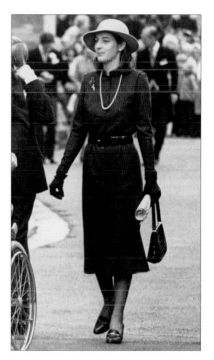

Above: Amanda Knatchbull, looking strikingly elegant at a State occasion. Her grandfather, Lord Mountbatten, wanted her to be Prince Charles's bride.

*Right: Lord Mountbatten
stands in front of his Irish
home, with his daughters and
eight grandchildren. Days later
he was assassinated by the IRA.
His grandson and a 16-year-
old boat boy died also.*

*Above and below: The funeral
was attended by many
politicians and European royals.
Prince Philip and Prince
Charles walk behind the coffin.*

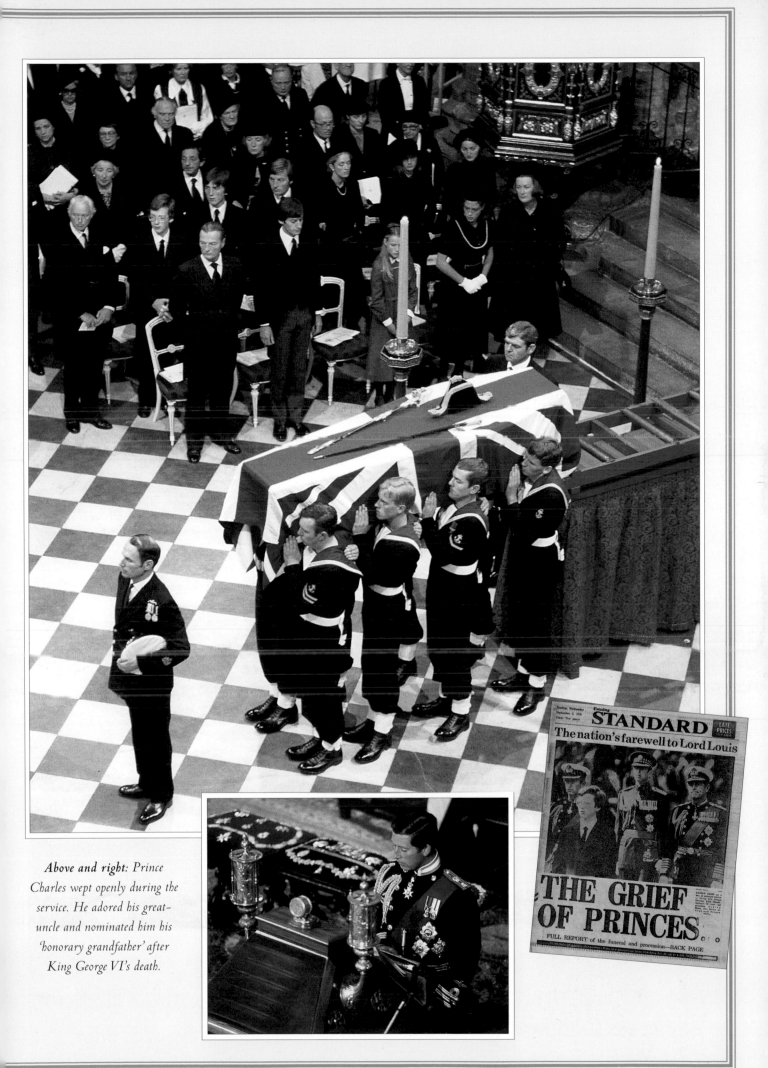

Above and right: Prince Charles wept openly during the service. He adored his great-uncle and nominated him his 'honorary grandfather' after King George VI's death.

The nation's farewell to Lord Louis

THE GRIEF OF PRINCES

FULL REPORT of the funeral and procession—BACK PAGE

Above: The Queen Mother and Lord Mountbatten were never comfortable together. She distrusted his attempts at matchmaking.

opponents they were – there was no warmth, no love lost.' Unlike Lord Mountbatten, Queen Elizabeth certainly did not believe in arranged marriages and was somewhat relieved when the relationship, such as it was, fizzled out after the Earl's assassination.

By now, no one in the Royal Family could escape the fact that there was a problem with Charles. The girls he fell for had been out in the world too long and if any one of them had been chosen as a bride, the media would have had a field day.

Contemporaries remember him at parties making a bee-line for the shapeliest girl in the room and if there was a lot of cleavage showing, so much the better. 'He was naturally drawn to the extrovert tart-with-a-heart type,' a friend recalls. 'He really appreciated girls who were warm-blooded, cosy and overtly sexy. But they had to be a good sort, a good sport and fun to be with but never in a Sloaney snobbish way.' His favourite party games were passing oranges under the chin and a naughty version of charades. 'The trouble was that Charles's lack of affection during childhood spilt over into adult life. He found it hard to overcome his natural reticence and form good relationships with the opposite sex. Although very close to his grandmother, the Queen Mother, he found younger women hard work. He would either jump on them or be too shy to go near them. That's why he preferred experienced, confident, often older, women, who would take the initiative', he adds.

Thus there was a sigh of relief at Clarence House when the Heir to the Throne, now over thirty, called round one day and confided to his grandmother that he wanted to marry Earl Spencer's youngest daughter, the nineteen-year-old Lady Diana. She seemed the answer to their prayers – beautiful, virginal and the offspring of a trusted royal friend. And the press and the people loved her. However, as a former aide remembers, 'Diana's grandmother Ruth, Lady Fermoy, the Queen Mother's chief lady-in-waiting, was completely against the match. She told the Queen Mother that she thought the couple were totally unsuited and that the marriage would end in tears. She strongly advised Queen Elizabeth to try to change Prince Charles's mind and dissuade him from going ahead with the proposal.'

But the Queen Mother was typically resolute in her reply. She told Lady Fermoy that she never gave advice unless it was asked for and that she thought Prince Charles was old enough and wise enough to make his own decision. 'If he is in love, and I think he is, and he wants to marry this girl then I will do all I can to help

Above: The Queen Mother with Prince Charles and Diana, Princess of Wales, in the happy early days of their marriage.

Opposite: Prince Charles is settled at last — the delighted families of the bride and groom gather for an official portrait.

him,' she said. The Queen Mother was as good as her word. She took Diana under her wing and installed her at Clarence House. A former member of the household remembers being told, 'Diana had terrible doubts on the eve of the marriage but the Queen Mother managed to reassure her. She was terribly sweet to Diana — very understanding and very sympathetic.' It was the same story when her younger grandson, Prince Andrew, came to marry. Then she looked after his fiancée, Sarah Ferguson, in the days before the marriage.

However the Queen Mother was not always the cuddly Grannie she appeared to be — there was an iron fist inside the velvet glove. A member of her household described her as 'a very strong and tough character. We loved her because she was absolutely firm in her views and never someone to cross.' The Queen Mother not only had famous tussles with Lord Mountbatten over Prince

Opposite: Prince Andrew's bride, Sarah Ferguson, with the Queen Mother at Ascot.

Charles but also with his nephew, the Duke of Edinburgh, over the way the monarchy should go. 'When the Queen came to the throne, the Duke was determined to modernize the Court,' recalls a senior courtier. 'The Queen Mother set her face against any reform or any change. She was frightened of what the Duke wanted to do. She thought, quite rightly as it has turned out, that by making the Royal Family more accessible, the mystery and respect surrounding the throne would be eroded. The harder the Duke pushed for change, the harder she applied the brakes. And the Queen was stuck in the middle. I remember the Queen once saying as we saw the car drawing up from Clarence House, "Well, that's where all the trouble is going to lie".'

The Duke and the Queen Mother were also at loggerheads over where Prince Charles should be sent to school. Both she and the Queen favoured Eton College, where all Queen Elizabeth's

Below: A rainy day at the races the Queen Mother, the Queen and Prince Philip wait for a winner.

Above: The picture of togetherness. Twenty-seven-year-old Prince Charles escorts the Queen Mother on her seventy-fifth birthday.

brothers had been. The Duke was determined that his son should go to his old school, Gordonstoun, as he felt 'the boy needed toughening up'. The argument raged back and forth but in the end it was the question of security that won the day. 'Eton is in a town and it was felt that there was a greater threat of kidnap than in a remote part of Scotland. In short, his parents thought he would be easier to protect if he went to Gordonstoun,' recalls a courtier.

It was a disaster. 'Prince Charles was completely shunned by the other boys who were afraid of being accused by their fellows of sucking up to the Heir to the Throne', recalls royal biographer Godfrey Talbot. 'He had a simply ghastly school life. He was miserable. It rather crushed him.' Instead of saying 'I told you so', Grannie went to see Prince Charles as often as she could and took him out for special treats. Even the Duke has admitted he was wrong. 'It is now acknowledged that he would have made friends if he had been sent to Eton because he would have been amongst his peers,' says a family member.

The Queen Mother's other grandchildren were never as close as Prince Charles had always been to Grannie. Princess Anne was a strong, resilient character who got on very well with her parents and led an independent and happy existence. Even her divorce from Captain Mark Phillips and subsequent marriage to Commander Tim Lawrence were handled with discretion and dignity. While the Queen Mother was quietly supportive, she was never called upon to play a major role in Anne's private life.

The Queen's younger children, Prince Andrew (born on 19 February 1960) and Prince Edward (born four years later on 10 March), were lucky enough to enjoy a very different relationship with their parents. Although Nanny was always there to supervise the daily routine, the Queen was now a mature parent and an established monarch. After missing so much of Charles and Anne's childhood, she was determined to play a bigger role in the upbringing of her younger offspring. Even the Duke had mellowed and, in any case, he found he had much more in common with his younger, more macho sons. Prince Andrew took liberties with his mother that would have made his elder brother's hair stand on end. Ever one for a practical joke, he put itching powder in the Queen's bed

Below: Four generations gather at Scrabster in Scotland for the summer holidays. Master Peter Phillips (centre) listens intently to great-grandmama.

and tampered with the royal television aerial. 'As you know the Queen is very keen on racing and once, when I was at the Palace, she turned on the television to watch one of her horses run,' recalls a friend. 'To her dismay, all we could see was a snowstorm. She was not amused and immediately summoned the engineer. He fiddled around for ages as she grew increasingly irritated. Finally, enter Prince Andrew with a big grin on his face. He thought the whole episode a great laugh and the Queen, after some protest, laughed with him.' The younger Princes always loved seeing Grannie — whether in London, Balmoral or Sandringham — but for them it was a more distant relationship.

Above: Stepping out in style, the Queen Mother is escorted by Prince Edward to a gala evening at the theatre.

The Queen Mother was in her eighties by the time Diana, Princess of Wales, came on the scene. During the early days with Prince Charles, Diana, like other members of the Royal Family, paid court to the old lady on high days and holidays but as the marriage hit trouble, she suspected that perhaps Queen Elizabeth was not quite the ally she had supposed.

As royal biographer, Andrew Morton observes, 'Diana saw her London home, Clarence House, as the fount of all negative comment about herself and her mother. She kept a distrustful distance from this matriarchal figure, describing social occasions hosted by the Queen Mother as stiff and overly formal … At the same time the Queen Mother … exercised an enormous influence over the Prince of Wales. It was a mutual adoration society from which Diana was effectively excluded.' 'The Queen Mother drives a wedge between Diana and the others,' noted a friend. 'As a result she makes every excuse to avoid her.'

It may be, however, that in the dying days of her marriage, the beleaguered Princess was being a little oversensitive. In the famous 'Squidgygate' tape, when a private conversation between Diana and her admirer James Gilbey was illicitly recorded by a radio ham, she talks about a 'strange look' the Queen Mother turned on her during lunch. 'It's not hatred, it's sort of interest and pity,' she said. Perhaps the Princess should have realized that there was more sympathy in that quarter than she imagined.

Even when the Queen Mother strongly disapproved, as she did when Diana and Fergie were photographed at Ascot pretending to poke men's bottoms with their umbrellas, she very rarely said anything. 'It was the long silences and what she *didn't* say, that really hit home,' observes a member of the household. 'That was when you knew you were in deep trouble.'

Today, events seem to have come full circle. Prince Charles is a single parent who has had to help Prince William and Prince Harry come to terms with their mother's tragic and untimely death. Even when she was in her one-hundredth year, Grannie was still there

Below: The Queen Mother exercised a great influence over Prince Charles but never gave advice unless it was asked for.

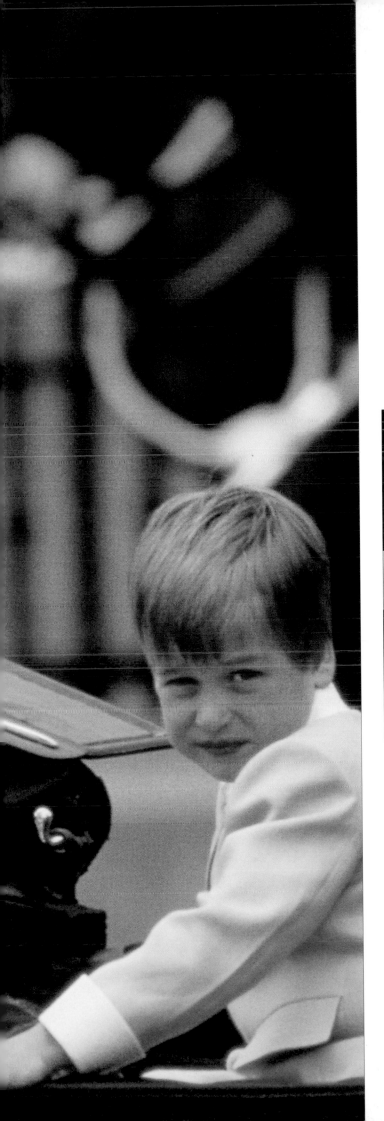

Opposite: The Queen Mother, Diana, Princess of Wales, and Prince William travel happily together in an open landau. However, in the dying days of her marriage, Diana saw the Queen Mother as an enemy and avoided her whenever possible. As a youngster, Prince William saw little of his great-grandmother.

Above: Diana, Princess of Wales, the Princess Royal, the Duchess of York and the Queen Mother watch solemnly as war veterans march past during the Service of Remembrance. The Queen Mother lost a brother and a nephew in the conflicts.

Below: As spry as ever: the Queen Mother flanked by Prince Charles and her great-grandsons Princes William and Harry during her ninety-seventh birthday celebrations at Clarence House.

to lend a hand. As a senior courtier notes, 'I think she was the one person that he could be with and not feel he was under scrutiny. He was totally relaxed in her company because he didn't feel he was being constantly assessed and judged the whole time. And I am sure that he told his grandmother things he would never dream of telling anyone else and consulted her about the boys. In the Queen Mother, he always found sympathy and understanding — someone prepared to listen and who was not constantly trying to give him advice. The way the Prince of Wales took his grand-mother's arm during the VE Day celebrations said everything about their relationship. It was a very special closeness indeed.'

Opposite: Prince William thoughtfully lends a hand as his Grannie leaves church, preceded by the Queen.

ON TOUR

From a very early age, the Queen Mother's character was such that she always felt an affinity and closeness to both her family and the people. The very small child who announced that her favourite hobby was 'liking people' was put in charge of showing guests at Glamis to their rooms as a young-ster. As she mounted the ancient stone spiral staircase, she would chatter away asking questions about their journey and pointing out items of interest. And when she was only four years old her mother, Lady Strathmore, once found her entertaining visitors to tea in the drawing-room, hav-ing rung for it herself, after they arrived early and she was else-where. One senior politician was startled when he was earnestly addressed by a pretty, little imp. Indicating an alcove off the drawing-room, she said, 'Shall us go and talk?' Their conversation, as far as he can remember, lasted for a full forty-five minutes.

When Elizabeth was a teenager, she mixed effortlessly with ordinary soldiers, many of them from overseas, whom she helped to nurse during the First World War. Later she

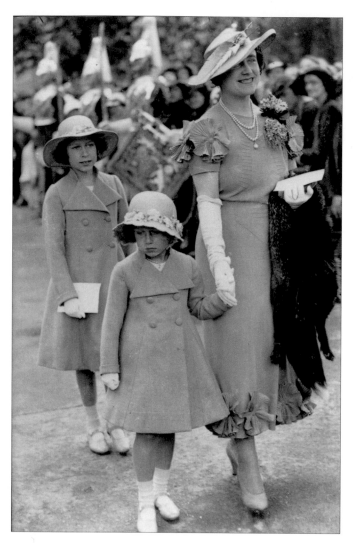

Above: Even as Duchess of York, and never thinking she would become Queen, she taught her daughters the art of 'mingling', an important part of the Royal Firm's job.

accompanied her mother on her visits to the sick and old on the family estate. She always had a ready and a friendly word for everyone. She gave her first speech at the age of fifteen, at a jumble sale, and confidently met the King's daughter, Princess Mary, at the head of her platoon of Girl Guides. She was over-awed by no one and loved by all.

Therefore, it comes as no surprise that when she married and became King George V's only daughter-in-law, she slid happily into her role of royal representative and public person. 'It was as if she had been doing it all her life,' one courtier remarked. The truth was that, in a sense, she had. She loved people, whoever they were or wherever they were from and, indeed, wherever she might have been.

Her first foreign adventure had been as a child when she visited her maternal grandmother, Mrs Scott, in a villa above Florence before the First World War. She and her younger brother, David, never forgot the excitement of travelling through Europe on the night train and she was thrilled by the bustle of a typical Italian station. In the care of their maiden aunt, Violet, the children were taken to see the Pitti Palace, the Boboli Gardens, the trecento frescos and the Medici tombs. It was a trip she never forgot and she was frequently to return to Italy in both a public and private capacity. Her second trip abroad came in her

Below: The Duke and Duchess of York in Australia. Many of the antipodeans, whom she had nursed during the First World War, were delighted to see her again.

early twenties when she went to visit her old friend Diamond Hardinge, the daughter of the British ambassador in Paris. The pair took in all the sights and went up the Eiffel Tower. There was also a good deal of shopping and giggling. Her second trip to Paris was a sadder one. Diamond was dying of tuberculosis and Elizabeth Bowes Lyon was one of her last visitors.

On her marriage into the Royal Family, Elizabeth's horizons broadened as she was called upon to travel widely throughout Britain and abroad. Everywhere she went, her charm and wit made her friends as she smoothed her shy husband's passage through public engagements.

Below: The King and Queen visit Canada before the Second World War. Her wit and charm made her friends wherever she went.

Above: *Feeling the heat during the South African tour of 1947. Queen Elizabeth invented the royal walkabout.*

Below: *Group Captain Peter Townsend, in the front passenger seat, was a firm favourite with the Royal Family but his friendship with Princess Margaret caused her heartache.*

Never was her tact more needed than during the tour of South Africa in 1947 when the royal couple and their daughters spent two months travelling – and indeed living – on the White Train as they journeyed through the country. At one stop a grizzled old Afrikaner who had fought in the Boer War pushed his way into the line of local officials to be presented. Equerries and ladies-in-waiting held their breath as he growled at the Queen, 'I can never forgive the English for what they did to my country.' After the briefest of pauses, the Bowes Lyon blue eyes flashed, as she sweetly replied, 'Oh I do understand. We in Scotland often feel very much the same.'

The reasons for the tour were threefold. The country's Prime Minister, Field Marshal Jan Smuts, the former Boer commander who fought so tenaciously against Queen Victoria, had come round to the view that monarchy could favourably influence public opinion and there was a general election coming up. The British Government felt such a visit would strengthen bonds with the Empire and Queen Elizabeth felt it would benefit her husband after the strain of the Second World War. It would also be a valuable experience

Above: Queen Elizabeth with that famous ostrich feather.

for sixteen-year-old Princess Margaret and her older sister – a foretaste of what would inevitably become a major feature of their official lives.

Although the King was to say that the trip had done him 'a great deal of good', he was often irritable in the heat and it was only his wife's enthusiasm that kept him going. The thirty-six nights on the train were indeed gruelling with a start at 6.30am when 'a black gentleman would come with a wet broom and start cleaning the windows,' and by the end of the journey he had lost a stone in weight.

In Oudtshoorn, 'the four of us' as the King called the Royal Firm, went to an ostrich farm. The King was expected to snip the tail feather off one of the unsuspecting birds but at the crucial moment there was a loud squawk and he accidentally took a quarter inch off its bottom. The ostrich, its head still in a canvas sack, began to quiver as did the King. Smiling serenely, Queen Elizabeth came forward and, taking the scissors, delicately snipped a piece of feather off its behind. 'We do a lot of gardening at home,' she explained to the assembled company. 'The King is good at digging and weeding but it is I who concentrate on the secateurs.'

Despite fears that the Royal Family might receive a cool reception, they were mobbed everywhere they went. Princess Margaret, already with a schoolgirl crush on her father's equerry, Group Captain Peter Townsend, was in fine form – her vivacity and 'presence' was not lost on the local press. Her older sister was described as shy and even grave – no doubt pining for her sweetheart Prince Philip whom she rang as often as possible from the White Train. However, she did rally, on the homeward bound leg of the journey, when, on her twenty-first birthday, she pledged that she would dedicate her whole life to the peoples of the Commonwealth, 'whether it be long or short.'

It was not Queen Elizabeth's first trip to Africa. During the first year of her marriage, repeated chest infections plagued her and schemes were suggested so that she could escape the bleak

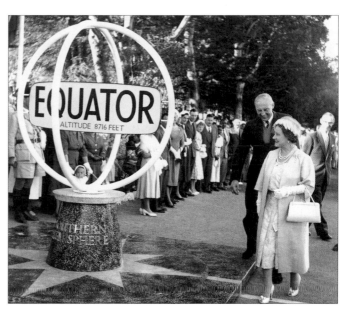

British winter. A journey to the heart of Africa was suggested, part official, part holiday. It was a thrilling prospect for someone who had spent her childhood pouring over the world atlas. Elizabeth and Bertie were all for the trip.

As they boarded the train bound for Marseilles on 1 December 1924, little did they realize that it was perhaps to be the greatest adventure of their lives and one they would never forget. Before they even arrived in Mombasa, Bertie had to undergo the double indignities of crossing the Equator twice, being shaved with a wooden razor and chucked into a tank of cold water.

Life was no less exciting as soon as they landed when they attended a ngoma or as one observer recorded, 'five thousand uncouthly bedizened natives dancing wildly for their delectation. As the participants had been prancing for three days their movements were by now somewhat rhythmically drunk and unorthodox. Some had gilt crowns bedecked with candles on their heads. In many cases a grass skirt was the only addition to the form in which they had been made. Tom-toms beat and horns howled.' As a memento the royal couple were given a gold coin on a red ribbon and an address thrust into the hollowed-out trunk of an elephant. Later they witnessed a march past of 12,000 Nubian warriors dressed only in monkey skins and attended a native parliament where the King invested King Daudi, the Kabaka of Buganda, with the KCMG.

Their trip was to take them through Kenya, Uganda and the Sudan, travelling 300 miles by train watching the game from a carriage in front of the engine, before embarking on a five-week safari. They were caught in a tropical storm in the middle of

Above. The Queen Mother at the Equator with Sir Evelyn Baring, Governor of Kenya, in 1959. Churchill persuaded her to come out of retirement after Bertie's death in 1952 because the country could not do without her.

A CENTURY OF TRAVEL

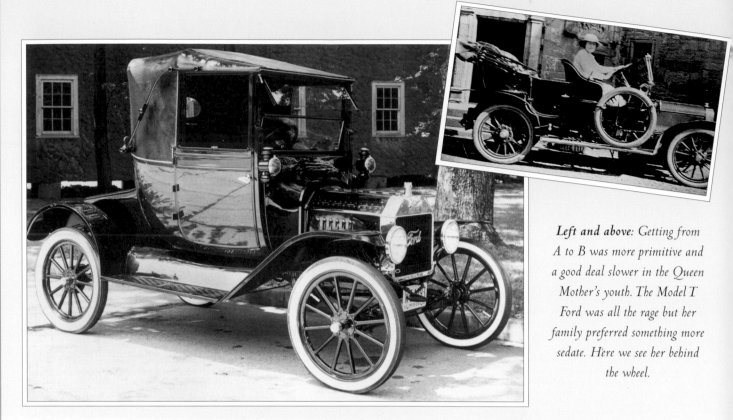

Left and above: Getting from A to B was more primitive and a good deal slower in the Queen Mother's youth. The Model T Ford was all the rage but her family preferred something more sedate. Here we see her behind the wheel.

Left: More than half a century later, the Queen Mother disembarks from Concorde.

Above: The pioneering Wright brothers at Kitty Hawk in 1900.

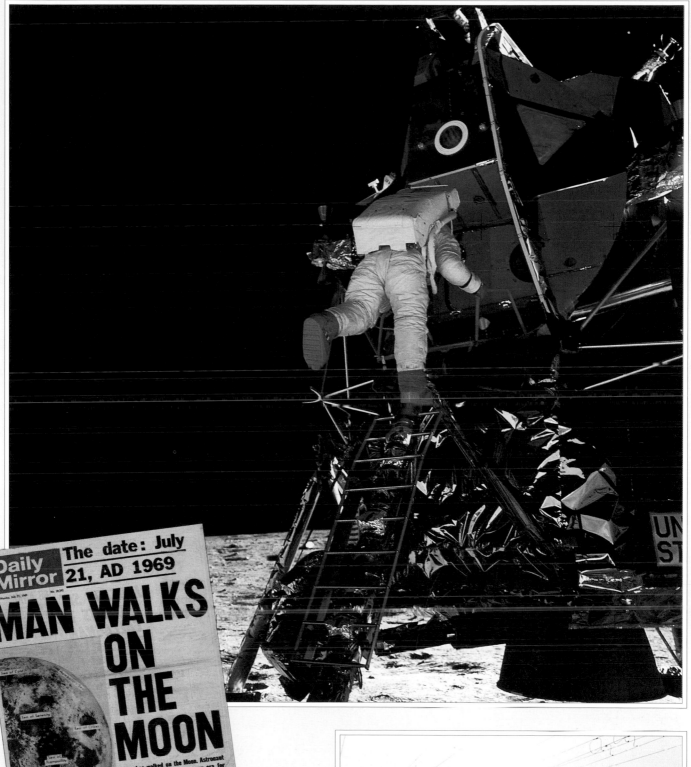

Above: A giant step for mankind as man walks on the moon in 1969. The Queen Mother, like the rest of the world, was riveted by the space mission.

Right: The Channel Tunnel. People had dreamed of a tunnel under the English channel since Elizabethan times. Now finally the triumph of engineering was achieved in the reign of Queen Elizabeth II, the Queen Mother's daughter.

Above: The Commonwealth was always very important to Queen Elizabeth and she took a keen interest in its affairs. On a visit to Rhodesia, now Zimbabwe, in 1960 she was welcomed by the Barotse people.

nowhere and seven of them had to pile into a Buick after one of the cars broke down in a river. They slept in little mud huts or under canvas or on the deck of a shallow draught steamer, which broke down. It was shades of the famous movie, *The African Queen* that was to star Katharine Hepburn and Humphrey Bogart in 1951. Elizabeth became an experienced hunter, shooting the plentiful game with a .275 Rigby, and went fishing on the Nile.

As her biographer David Duff records, 'Everywhere she had travelled her courage and tenacity had been admired. She had trekked fifteen miles and more at a stretch. She had been up to her waist in mud and water. She had helped put up her tent when it blew down and dried out her sodden clothes. She had shot for her supper. The praise, and the smile, of her echoed back from Mombasa and Nairobi, Entebbe and Khartoum.' It was a sentiment that was often to be repeated during the next seventy-five years.

The Queen Mother's warmth and regal informality was to become the template for her family on official duties. It was in Canada, just before the Second World War, that she first invented the royal walkabout. To the amazement of American newspaper men and the horror of her security guards, she plunged into a sea of 10,000 tough First World War veterans when she was unveiling a war memorial in Ottawa.

Above: The Queen Mother looking as glamorous and stylish as ever during the 1960 tour of Rhodesia, now Zimbabwe. Her stamina was legendary and she exhausted staff many years her junior.

Her five-foot-two frame disappeared in the throng as she was swamped by soldiers who well remembered her kindness and compassion to the wounded at Glamis. Perspiration poured from the protection squad as they struggled to keep in contact with their charge whom they could not even see. However, the Queen Mother was delighted with the experience. As banner headlines proclaimed that she had taken a risk that no other President or monarch would contemplate, her observation was merely that, 'Canada is so … so uplifting.'

She also gave her detectives heart failure by breaking away from the official programme. While laying a foundation stone, she heard the nearby burr of the Highland tongue. Realizing that many of the masons working on the building were from her native Scotland, she broke away from the group of Canadian dignitaries and marched purposefully towards them, Bertie following in her wake. As

Below: Meeting the people of Rhodesia, now Zimbabwe. Queen Elizabeth had the knack of making everyone she talked to feel the most important person in the world.

70,000 astonished spectators looked on, she stood laughing and joking with the workmen as they swapped stories of home. Such behaviour broke all the rules of royal precedent but it was a style that succeeding generations would emulate, most notably Diana, Princess of Wales, more than forty years later. It was no coincidence that, half a century on, it was to Canada that the Queen Mother returned, in her eighty-ninth year, for her last major foreign tour.

It was June 1939, when she left the United States of America for the last time before the Second World War, that the Queen Mother was first dubbed 'The Queen of Hearts', a mantle that Diana was also to adopt. Her famous smile and tireless energy attracted crowds of three million or more as she took the country by storm. More unfamiliar compliments were paid to her. She was described as 'A Cute Trick' and President Franklin Roosevelt confided to her husband, 'My, you're a great Queen picker!' When she returned to the country as a widow, it was the same story. As the *World-Telegram* commented, 'The royal lady with the peaches-and-cream complexion and the twinkling orbs not only drew a record crowd of 2,800 smart-setters to the Waldorf-Astoria ballroom; she sent them away humming "God Save the Queen" like a first-night audience whistling the top tunes of the hit show.' African American children, who she visited in Harlem, said she was 'A Wow' and everyone agreed. However, her tremendous popularity could have its drawbacks. When she tried to go shopping at Saks, the

Above and opposite: The Queen Mother revisits Canada in her eighties on her last major foreign tour. The country, she said, was just 'so . . . so uplifting.'

Below: The King and Queen are mobbed during a visit to America in 1939. She became a close friend of President Franklin Roosevelt and his wife Eleanor and did much for Anglo-American relations.

Above: The Queen Mother in Australia in 1958. It was once suggested that she would make an excellent Governor-General. 'I am afraid not,' replied the Queen firmly. 'We could not possibly spare Mummy.'

department store in New York, she had to rocket up and down in the lift to evade a pack of puffing well-wishers. Despite the pursuit, she managed to buy presents for her grandchildren, a magnetic bottle-opener and a game of Scrabble, for herself.

It was not the first time that a royal tour had taken on a slightly ludicrous note. One of Princess Margaret's private secretaries recalls the Queen Mother telling a story about when she and the Princess were visiting an exhibition in South Africa. When it was over, their host duly bowed low as she thanked him for such an interesting tour. As the doors slammed shut, the car pulled slowly away and the Queen Mother started to wave to the crowds of well-wishers. The official was still walking alongside. 'What a nice man,' she commented, 'seeing us off so kindly.'

The next time she glanced out, the man was still there, now trotting, waving and looking a little flushed. As the Rolls picked up speed, the man continued to keep pace, waving wildly and starting to go purple in the face. 'If he's not careful,' said the Queen Mother, 'he'll give himself a heart attack.' Then the penny dropped. The cavalcade came to an abrupt halt and the tie of the half-throttled official was extricated from the door. With typical thoughtfulness, enquiries were later made to ensure that the man was none the worse for his experience.

There were other slightly silly moments, when the Queen Mother visited Venice in her mid-eighties. Since childhood she had seen 'Serenissima' as a distant vision from the train carrying her south to Florence. Now, she determined that at last she would see the place for herself. Her devoted daughter, the Queen, lent the Royal Yacht *Britannia* and a jolly party set off. The most important and difficult function for the British Embassy officials was to ensure that the Queen Mother had the racing paper, *The Sporting Life*, on her breakfast table every morning. Her staff, it was explained, needed to know how their fancied horses were doing. There was clearly, too, a hot line to a friendly bookie. As the Queen Mother wondered at the glories of St Mark's Cathedral, one member of her household was

Below: The Queen Mother in St Mark's Square, Venice. As a child, she had glimpsed the city from a train but it was not until her eighties that she was able to see its full glories for herself.

Above: The Queen Mother delights in a gondola ride just before a surprise but unwelcome gift gives her security guards the jitters.

sadly seen tearing up betting slips after the voice in his ear-piece had informed him that his horses had lost.

An extraordinary incident was to take place during the trip. By popular request, the Queen Mother agreed to vary the official programme and take an unscheduled gondola ride on the canals. Surrounded by gondola 'gun ships', packed full of security officers armed with the latest and most powerful sub-machine-guns, she set sail. However, no one in the last-minute arrangements had banked on the low bridges and the stature of the *Star* newspaper's royal correspondent, one Andrew Morton. Well over six feet in his stockinged feet and rightly named 'Superman' by his fellow journalists, he bent as low as he could as she passed under a bridge and passed her 'One Cornetto'. The Queen Mother looked at the ice-cream with surprise, before it was grabbed from her grasp by royal staff, passed like a bomb down the line of officials and thrown to the unsuspecting security men. Everyone had their headline.

Significantly, one of her visitors on board the Royal Yacht was Dame Freya Stark, a pioneering voyager who had journeyed alone through Arabia in the 1930s. The Queen Mother, too, loved to travel and became the first member of the Royal Family, although the oldest of the 'Royal Firm', to circumnavigate the world exclusively by air. While top executives complain of jet lag, her stamina was legendary. 'Her powers of recovery after even the toughest tour were remarkable,' says an aide. 'It took her about six hours.' On one occasion she bettered this – arriving at the races only three hours after landing from a transatlantic flight.

Her great friend Lord St John of Fawsley well remembers her trip to Venice. 'We had had an incredibly tiring day visiting Torcello and in the evening there was to be a reception on the Royal Yacht. The rest of us were exhausted, but there she was greeting every single one of the three hundred guests. By the end of the party, I was slumped in a corner – but to my amazement, I saw Queen Elizabeth saying goodbye to all those same visitors.'

Another friend recalls a visit to her couturier. 'I remember when she came for a fitting after a long tiring afternoon visiting the Chelsea pensioners. She was asked if she would like to sit down and rest for a moment. 'Oh, no,' she replied. 'I am quite fresh, thank you, but I *did* feel sorry for those poor, dear, *old* gentlemen.' Their average age was a mere seventy-five and she was over ninety.

The Queen Mother's clothes have been admired and copied

Below: As spritely as ever, the Queen Mother meets war veterans. She said she felt sorry for 'those poor, dear, old gentlemen' although she was nearly twenty years their senior.

Below: Fifty years on and not a day older. The Queen Mother chats to Prime Minister John Major during the VE Day celebrations. Although non-political, she always took a lively and knowledgeable interest in current affairs.

everywhere but it was on a visit to France that she became a fashion icon. The tour had been postponed due to her mother, Lady Strathmore's death, and the royal designer Sir Norman Hartnell, had just two weeks to change all her outfits to white, one of the colours of mourning.

According to George Mitchison, former managing director of the House of Hartnell, it was her husband, King George VI, who was the inspiration behind the wonderful creations that were to evolve into her distinctive style of dress. 'The King took Sir Norman into the picture gallery at Buckingham Palace and, stopping under the famous Winterhalter portrait of Queen Victoria and her family, he pointed at the wonderful crinolines and said, "That is how I would like my wife to be dressed."'

The fashion-conscious French were bowled over and hundreds of column inches of newsprint were devoted to her dresses. And if they liked her clothes, the Parisians were no less rapturous about her person. 'Today France is a monarchy again,' screamed the headlines. 'We have taken Elizabeth to our hearts. She rules over two nations.' However, seeing how much she helped her shy husband, they could not resist a little joke at their expense. The Queen Mother was dubbed 'soutien-George', meaning George's support. ('Soutien-gorge' is French for bra.)

'Her style really evolved from there,' says Mr Mitchison. 'She always favoured pastel colours, not only because pink and blue happened to be her favourites, but so she could easily be seen in

Above: 'That is how I would like my wife to be dressed,' said King George VI after frog-marching designer Sir Norman Hartnell into the picture gallery at Buckingham Palace. The Winterhalter-inspired designs turned Queen Elizabeth into the fashion icon of her time.

Above: All her life the Queen Mother was drawn to 'ordinary' people. Here she chats to workers at the National Theatre.

the crowd. And she loved embroideries on the ball gowns we made for banquets and special State dinners. She used to explain that if she was sitting next to someone who was rather shy, she could use the embroidery as a talking point to get the conversation going. Her Majesty was a very discriminating customer. She had a firm idea of what she wanted and we had to produce a lot of sketches. If she were going abroad, the outfits had to match the colour of the ribbon of whatever decoration she would be wearing and the dresses designed accordingly. I remember she used to point to a sketch and say, "Ah, I see there is room for a little tinkle there," meaning a brooch or a small piece of jewellery.'

In Britain, the Queen Mother always brought a touch of magic to whatever she did, although old age prevented her from fulfilling the number of engagements she did in past years. The occasion, in 1987, will always be remembered when she turned the apparently dull task of viewing building developments in the regenerated Docklands area into a triumph of public relations. Since the days of the Blitz, she always loved the East-Enders and delighted in the atmosphere of a Cockney afternoon. So when

Opposite: Queen Elizabeth's mother, Lady Strathmore, was famous throughout Scotland for her wonderful hats. Her youngest daughter followed in her footsteps.

Left: She may have been a royal favourite but so were they. The Queen Mother greets the Pearly Kings and Queens of her beloved East End before taking a drop of rum in her tea, in the icy early hours, as she tours Smithfield market.

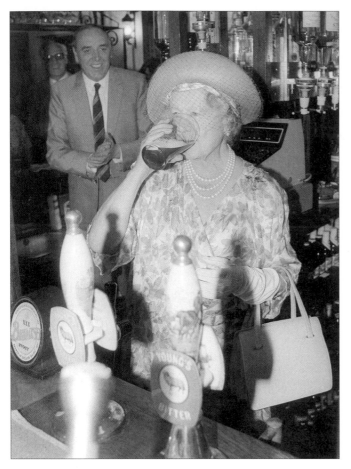

Above: The landlord offered her champagne, but the Queen Mother insisted that she would prefer a pint when she dropped in for a 'quick one' on her way home.

her official duties were over, she instructed her chauffeur to stop outside the Queen's Head, a popular Stepney pub and marched inside, surrounded by her entourage. The landlord and his customers did a double take as the familiar figure burst through the doors of the saloon bar. As soon as he had recovered his wits, the landlord offered her a glass of champagne. With the famous smile that won her fans around the world, she declined his kind gesture. 'No, thank you,' she replied. 'Might I have a pint of bitter, please?'

For many years the Queen Mother was Chancellor of the University of London and one year it fell to the President of the Union to lead her onto the dance floor for the first waltz. The poor young man, who had two left feet, had taken a crash course in dancing lessons but the strain of the occasion took its toll. As he lumbered round the floor, sweating profusely, he found himself kicking his Chancellor all over the place. With a bright smile, and ignoring her crushed toes, the Queen Mother put him at ease and said, 'Don't worry, Mr President, you haven't knocked my tiara off yet.'

Below: The Queen Mother dances with the head of the Students' Union, who trod on her feet. Even the radical Trotskyites of London University put their political views aside when their Chancellor of twenty-five years came to visit.

The Queen Mother was never one to stand on ceremony. On another occasion, she was invited for drinks at the university and to her host's horror, it was discovered there were no tongs for the ice bucket when she asked for a gin and tonic. With a smile and a twinkle in her eye, she said, 'Oh, Mr President, don't worry — we can manage like this' and putting her hand in the ice bucket, she extracted two cubes and dropped them into her glass.

None of her friends will ever forget the time when they were watching the racing in the royal box and the National Anthem struck up on the television. Her companions started rising to their feet but the Queen Mother waved them to stay put. 'Oh, do turn the set off,' she said. 'Unless one is actually there, it's rather

Above: The Women's Institute fair at Sandringham. Queen Elizabeth was their strongest supporter and, true Scotswoman that she was, never missed the chance to pick up a bargain to give to her great-grandchildren.

out of place and embarrassing, don't you think? Rather like hearing the Lord's Prayer whilst one is playing canasta!'

The Queen Mother was a public figure for over seventy-five years but she never lost the knack of making people feel that she was just one of them. Not only was she adored by the public but she had a lifelong love affair with the press. Unlike some other members of the family, she realized that reporters and photographers have a job to do and she made things as easy as possible for them. Many remember the old days when she would deliberately lead the King to a spot where there was the best possible backdrop and all recall her many kindnesses.

On one occasion a stray dog joined her on a platform and she bent down to stroke it. One photographer was reloading his camera and missed the shot. Seeing his distress, she called the dog back and did it all over again. Another time a petty official was pushing a photographer aside. 'Please don't do that,' she called. 'Mr So-and-So is an old friend of mine and we both have work to do.' However, perhaps one of the nicest stories is that told by

Right: Both the Dalai Lama and Queen Elizabeth inspired a nation. 'Duty is the rent you pay for life,' Queen Elizabeth was told as a child. She never forgot that message and nor has the Dalai Lama. It seemed that the pair had much in common.

royal photographer Ian Showell. 'I was the first man on duty out-side Clarence House the day Lady Diana Spencer left the Queen Mother's home to marry Prince Charles. Shortly after I arrived at 4.30am, I noticed one of the curtains twitch at one of the win-dows inside the house. Soon afterwards, a uniformed footman came marching towards me bearing a silver salver laden with a teapot, a cup made of the finest royal china, plus milk and sugar, with the compliments of the Queen Mother. At that time in the morning, the tea tasted like nectar.'

Above: Three Knights of the Garter. King Badouin of the Belgians (left) with the Queen Mother and the Duke of Kent. Queen Elizabeth strongly supported the liberal view of equality for all but was at heart deeply conservative.

CHAPTER SIX

A LIFE WELL-LIVED

Opposite: The Queen Mother poses in her drawing-room for Anthony Crickmay, surrounded by photographs of her friends and family. A childhood portrait of her eldest daughter, the Queen, hangs on a wall behind her.

The Queen Mother's legendary sense of fun frequently enabled her to use humour to dispel many an awkward situation. This was never truer than during a family holiday north of the border, as one of her great-nieces remembers.

It was a cold, wet day in August. For what seemed like weeks the rain had been teeming down in Scotland and the grouse shooting season had been wiped out. With no guests at Balmoral because there were no birds to shoot, the family kicked its heels and waited for more clement times. An air of boredom and frustration hung over the castle. Then the Queen suggested that despite the weather, they might have a picnic in one of the royal lodges built by Queen Victoria and her Consort Prince Albert. The idea was enthusiastically embraced and instructions were given that hampers, dogs and children should be got ready.

Right: The Queen Mother loved the log cabin given to her as a present and built on her Scottish estate at Birkhall. It has been the scene of many a jolly picnic.

Above: The Queen Mother takes Prince Charles's arm, while Prince Andrew shares a joke with Princess Anne, and Prince Edward holds his mother's hand as the Royal Family walk to church at Sandringham.

Light Infantry and the Royal Scots Fusiliers. Princess Margaret was naturally the guest of honour and we were sitting sedately at the high table. Suddenly a soldier, made bolder by a large quantity of whisky, came reeling out of the gloom towards us. It was quite plain that he was intent on addressing the Princess and was bound to say something ghastly. I had to do something about it and on the spur of the moment, I bellowed: "Go away and sit down." Luckily that deterred him and he went swaying off in the opposite direction. Princess Margaret turned to me with the sweetest of smiles and said, "Goodness me – the Queen is always saying that to her corgis and they never take any notice!"'

The Princess was not above pulling the leg of her 'Jocks' as she called her Scottish regiment. When inspecting a parade she would often speak to one of the men. The reply would invariably conclude with the words, 'yes, Sir'. 'But I am not Sir', she would tease, 'I am Ma'am.' Again, the flummoxed soldier would respond, 'yes, Sir'. She was always very amused by that.

Above: No matter what the weather, the Queen Mother, hardy Scottish lass that she was, enjoyed a brisk walk with her dogs.

The exchange was typical of the Princess and led to her mother's 'slightly eyebrows raised' attitude to her gifted younger daughter. 'The Queen Mother was only too aware that if they were, say, taking the salute at a military parade, Margaret would be standing very regally at her side but her sparkling eyes would be flirting with the chaps', explains a former courtier. 'This led to a very affectionate but rather distant relationship.' Her mother was also adept at handling the Princess's moods. Once, during a fire practice at Royal Lodge in

Left: The Queen Mother's Aberdeenshire residence, Birkhall. She is said to have left it to Prince Charles.

Windsor Great Park, the Princess refused to get out of bed for a mock drill. The staff were dithering about what to do when they spotted the Queen Mother drifting down the stairs in swirls of chiffon. When told of the dilemma, she replied with a laugh,' Oh well, she'll just have to burn then, won't she.'

Both the Queen Mother and the Queen shared the same conservative standards and, despite a heavy load of public duties, centred their lives round the family. The Queen's face in repose can look rather severe but, as any of her courtiers will tell you, she is full of fun and an excellent mimic of the pretentious or pompous. She and her mother used to speak on the telephone every day and saw each other as often as their diaries allowed. 'The Queen loved her mother very much and she was frightfully important to her,' explains a former courtier. 'They had the same slightly mischievous sense of humour and laughed at the same things. They always had fun together and shared the same interests, like racing.

They both loved the outdoor, country sort of life and preferred a long walk with the dogs to the social whirl. Because they had such a happy, secure childhood, the Queen Mother was very close to both her daughters and they were very fond of and loyal to each other,' he adds. 'And as some people have found to their cost, if you crossed one, you crossed them all.'

It was once suggested that the Queen Mother might be a very suitable candidate for Governor-General of Australia. The Queen was adamant. 'Oh no, I'm afraid not. We could not possibly spare Mummy.'

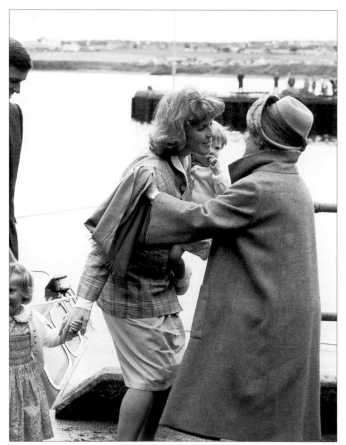

Below: Welcoming the family ashore from the Royal Yacht Britannia. *The Queen Mother embraces Sarah, Duchess of York, seen here with Princesses Beatrice and Eugenie.*

Never was this truer than when scandal touched the Queen for the only time in her reign. According to the famous correspondent Alistair Cooke, reporting from New York in February 1957, 'Not since the first rumours of a romance between the former King Edward VIII and the then Mrs Simpson have Americans gobbled up the London dispatches quite so avidly as they have been doing since Friday afternoon. For two days and nights the tabloid press and the evening papers from coast to coast have waved banner headlines over a story from London, first cabled to this country by the *Baltimore Sun*'s London bureau, reporting a "rift" in the marriage of the Queen and the Duke of Edinburgh.' Unidentified members of café society were said to be 'talking openly' of an estrangement between the couple as Prince Philip made his way home following a four-month tour. 'Within twenty-

Above: Mother and daughter: the Queen Mother embraces the Queen. The pair were very close and spoke on the telephone daily.

Opposite: As sprightly
as ever, the Queen
Mother poses in her
wonderful garden for
a seventieth birthday
portrait by Cecil
Beaton.

four hours the Palace brushed off the rumour as "totally untrue",'
continues Mr Cooke in his report. 'This prompt disclaimer was
a disappointment to the scandal sniffers. But since the press here
is united in the practising belief that where there's smoke, there's
fire, no foreign news editor – from the most scurrilous to the
most responsible – could ignore the story. Consequently the cables
went out asking for "follow-up" stories. The only new surprise
is the fact, which is the burden of today's dispatches, that the
British press has by instinct or command submitted itself to a
general gag.'

As a former member of the household recalls, 'The Americans
thought they were on to a good thing. They had broken the news
of Edward's love affair with Wallis, while the British kept mum,
and they thought the same thing was happening again.
Unfortunately on this occasion, they could not have been more
wrong. I was with the Queen at the time and she seemed not
unduly fussed. In fact we made a few jokes about it. She realized,
like the rest of us, that while the Duke, like every man in the
world, loves a pretty face, things would never go beyond a gentle
flirtation. As ever the Queen Mother was a tower of strength and
advised the Queen to ignore the "silly rumours". She said it was
very sad that some people had nothing better to do than indulge
in idle gossip and hurt others. She was very protective and anxious that her daughter should not be hurt.'

Instead, with a supportive Princess Margaret at her side, the
Queen Mother took the Queen off to enjoy a day's racing. 'She
was determined that the family would present a united front and
demonstrate how ludicrous the rumours were. Her judgement as
ever was impeccable,' he adds.

Five days later the Duke was bounding up the steps of an air-
liner, two at a time, to welcome his wife to Portugal. In the words
of the *Sunday Express*, 'For two and a half minutes they greeted
each other alone in a special compartment with the blinds drawn.
Then they came out into the afternoon sunshine. The Queen was

TWENTIETH-CENTURY WOMEN

Right: It was a long, hard struggle but Emmeline Pankhurst did not give up the fight for women's suffrage. With her two daughters, Christabel and Sylvia, she faced jail to win the vote for women and is seen here leaving Bow Street.

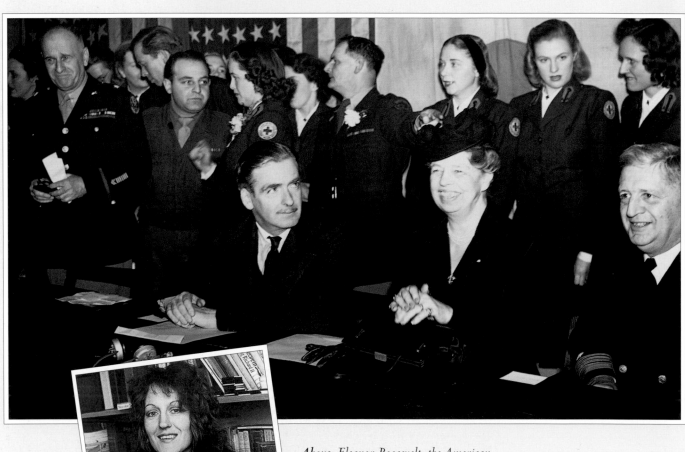

Above: Eleanor Roosevelt, the American President's wife, with British Prime Minister Sir Anthony Eden. She became a good friend to Britain and the Queen Mother.

Left: Germaine Greer, author of the acclaimed book The Female Eunuch, which proved to be a seminal work on feminist issues.

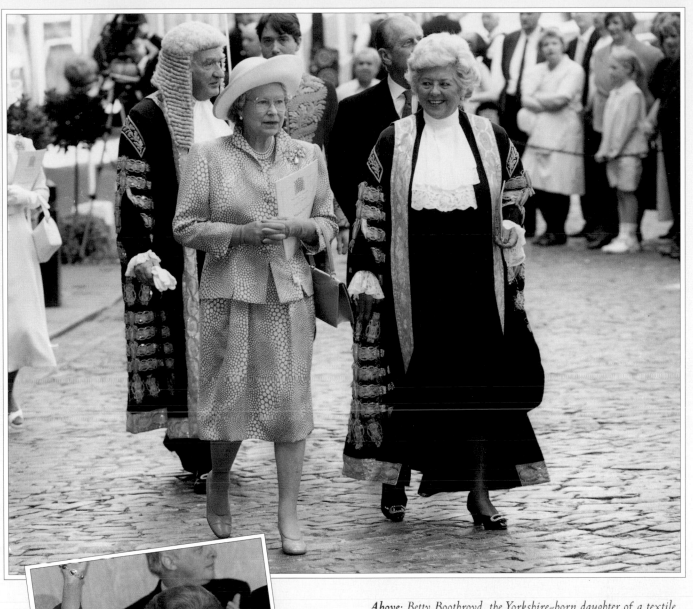

Above: Betty Boothroyd, the Yorkshire-born daughter of a textile worker and weaver, became the first woman Speaker in the House of Commons in 1992.

Above and right: Britain had its first female Prime Minister with Margaret Thatcher in 1979. Tony Blair's Labour victory in 1997 proved yet further the changes in politics as over 50 women formed part of the new government.

radiant. The Duke was smiling broadly. And on his tanned face was a tiny smear of lipstick.' Others noted that he was wearing a tie covered with hearts. All was well.

When Princess Margaret broke up with Lord Snowdon, she turned to her mother for help but found Queen Elizabeth even more distressed than she was. The terrible rows that went on into the early hours of the morning followed by days of silent sulks had taken their toll. The Queen Mother was very fond of Lord Snowdon and was upset when the couple finally parted. Also she worried at the depressed state of her daughter and was therefore pleased, although slightly surprised, when the Princess found solace in the company of Roddy Llewellyn, fifteen years her junior.

Roddy was fond of entertaining the Princess at his commune in Wiltshire where upper class hippies emulated the 'good life'. The old Etonian, as the Princess's pet, was in turn invited to her mother's country home, Royal Lodge. One day the Queen Mother came face to face with the young man, wearing nothing but a pair of underpants, in a corridor. 'Oh, frightfully sorry, Ma'am' he apologized. 'I was just looking for nanny to see if she would be very kind and sew a button on this shirt.' The Queen Mother sailed majestically on.

The Queen Mother was always a marvellous and generous hostess. The food she served was always of the best and the wines, the finest. Friends used to look forward to an invitation to any of her homes because it was always tremendous fun, if at times a trifle exhausting. One guest remembers a dinner party at Royal Lodge. 'It was well past midnight and I had to get up at six the following morning to go to work. The party was still in full swing and Queen Elizabeth was on sparkling form. Toast after toast was being drunk, the raconteurs were in full flow and there were plenty of singsongs going on. I leant across the table and whispered to one of the ladies-in-waiting, "Do you think we might be going to bed soon?" "Have I got news for you," she replied.

Right: An accomplished
pianist, the Queen
Mother was the star of
the show at a school
concert. She was always
happy to play for the
entertainment of family
and friends.

Right: An accomplished pianist, the Queen Mother was the star of the show at a school concert. She was always happy to play for the entertainment of family and friends.

'This could go on until four in the morning." "Oh, my God," I gasped. "It'll kill me."'

According to one of her relations, the Queen Mother had an interesting attitude to drink. 'She did not consider champagne to be alcoholic and used it as a pick-me-up. She normally had one or two stiff gin-and-its before she set out on an engagement and wine with her meals. She was really incredible. Drink seemed to have no effect on her at all.' Others too, she felt, should be fortified before official functions. One organizer was amazed when, shortly before they were due to take to the public stage, she proffered him her glass and said, 'Take a gulp.' While the Queen Mother seemed to be always in the pink, some people occasionally felt a little bit the worse for wear the morning after. However help was at hand. A discreet little chemist's just up the road in St James's had a magic potion – commonly known as 'The Royal Hangover Cure'. The recipe was naturally secret.

Opposite: Her former son-in-law, Lord Snowdon, captured the radiance and warmth of the Queen Mother. Despite the divorce from Princess Margaret, the pair were on excellent terms.

At Royal Lodge there used to be lively musical soirées at which the Queen Mother herself was known to perform. Accompanied by Lord Hailsham she would think nothing of singing popular songs like 'Sur le Pont d'Avignon' and 'My Old Man Said Follow the Van' as a duet with Noel Coward. She was fond of the theatrical world and often entertained artists she admired at her London home, Clarence House. The opera superstar Luciano Pavarotti once dined with her. At the time he stated that, 'When I meet this lady, it is always such a great pleasure. She is the greatest lady in the world and I adore her.'

The artist Sir Hugh Casson visited her Sandringham home. 'There was a picnic on the beach at Hockham. The footmen brought up all the hampers and she unpacked them herself and set out all the food. After lunch she took the dogs for a walk. Not everyone went with her – some found it a little too brisk but she never seemed to

Below: The Queen Mother dishes out Good Boy Choc-drops to the corgis.

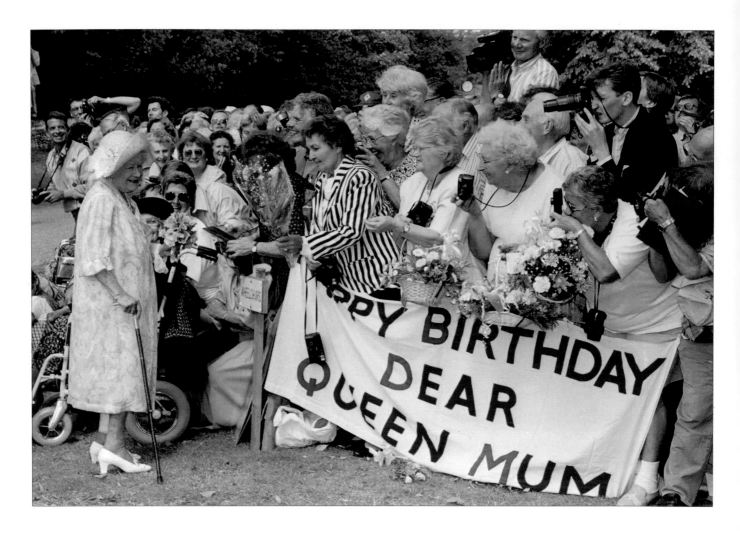

Above: What she did best; greeting the crowds during her annual birthday walkabout. The Queen Mother had a kind word for everyone.

notice the cold.' The Queen Mother always loved her dogs and she was often seen with her corgis sitting in an orderly circle around her. She used to give each dog in turn a Good Boy Choc-drop, saying, 'One for you, and one for you, and one for you ...' And when she had completed the circle, she popped one into her own mouth, with the words, 'And one for me.'

The Queen Mother liked anything that made her laugh. One friend recalls an evening when the guests arrived terribly late. As they rushed in full of apologies, she replied, 'No, no, please don't be sorry. I was glad you were late because it gave me a chance to see *Dad's Army* again.'

The Queen Mother's stamina and tirelessness were legendary. According to Lord St John of Fawsley, nobody ever looked at their watch in her presence – to do so would have been a mortal sin. 'If all was going well and everyone was enjoying themselves, time didn't matter,' he explained. 'You never mentioned time in the Queen Mother's presence.'

Despite two hip operations, the Queen Mother's incredible energy remained undiminished. On her ninety-eighth birthday she walked for fifty minutes greeting the crowds of well-wishers and accepting bouquets. As ever she had a kind word for everyone including one little six-year-old who blurted out, 'I have met your daughter and do you know, she is the *Queen!*' 'Yes, I know,' replied the Queen Mother. 'Isn't it exciting!'

Apart from her family, the Queen Mother had two great passions in her life – fishing and racing. In both she scored many triumphs, landing prize fish from New Zealand to Scotland and winning many of the classic races. About the only race to elude her was the Grand National. Once she came very close, but her horse Devon Loch mysteriously collapsed with a clear lead only yards from the finish line. Although she reluctantly had to give up fishing in her eighties, she continued to love nothing more than a day at the races surrounded by friends, many of them relying on her expert advice when chancing a flutter.

Below: One that did not get away. The Queen Mother fishing during the New Zealand tour of 1927. She adored the sport and did not give it up until she was in her eighties.

Above: Queen Elizabeth, the Queen Mother, leaves hospital after a hip operation. She was said to be a model patient.

Above: The Queen Mother with Andrew Parker-Bowles, Camilla's ex-husband. She had a passion for racing and liked to keep up-to-date with weighing-room gossip.

Below: The Queen Mother was a successful owner and loved nothing better than having a winner — especially when the cup was presented by the Queen.

Every year she used to host racing weekends at Royal Lodge for one of her favourite events of the racing calendar, the King George VI and Queen Elizabeth Diamond Stakes at Ascot. 'It was all very jolly,' says her cousin. 'We arrived on Friday evening in time for drinks and went racing all day Saturday. On Sunday we talked, or played bridge or racing demon. If the weather was fine, a game of croquet might have been suggested.'

Although the Queen Mother never bet on a horse, her long-time private secretary Sir Martin Gilliat used to love a flutter. It was an in-joke that whenever he backed a loser, he would turn to his employer and say, 'Well, there goes the car — we'll just have to go home by bus!'

The Queen Mother liked to keep up with weighing-room gossip and she was very loyal to her racing friends. One of her trainers, Nicky Henderson, recalls a dash to Clarence House so the Queen Mother would not miss a race. 'She was at luncheon at the Savoy where I had the honour of sitting next to her. I had a runner in the 3.10 at Fontwell Park and she quietly ventured, "Do you think we will be able to slip away in time to watch the horse? If you'd like to follow me …" I had visions of the royal party trooping into a betting shop, but no. I made my exit at 2.55 and jumped into a taxi I'd lined up earlier. When I told the cabbie, "Follow that Rolls", he thought he had landed a part in a film. We hurtled round Eros at about eighty miles an hour and

Opposite: The Queen Mother and the Queen delight in a day's racing at Royal Epsom. The Queen has inherited her mother's expert eye when it comes to horseflesh.

Above: A keen theatre-goer, the Queen Mother meets the cast of The Pirates of Penzance.

screeched through the gates at Clarence House. We rushed in, up the stairs, just in time to see the race on the satellite system. I only hope that I can move that smartly when I am ninety-four.'

Since childhood the Queen Mother had a great love of thespians. According to a former actor she would ask if she might come down to the set while filming was going on. Therefore, she was on hand when *On Her Majesty's Secret Service* was being shot at Elstree. James Villiers, who was playing M to George Lazenby's Bond, was among the throng who showed the Queen Mother round the set. The actor is distantly related to the royal family and was there when he thought one of the cast was rude to her. With her usual aplomb, the Queen Mother shrugged off the incident, but he bellowed at the unfortunate individual, 'If twenty-four people die and I become King, I will have you beheaded.'

In the world of pictures, the Queen Mother, so carefully groomed by her artistic mother, was advanced by royal standards. She collected modern paintings. It was a great bond she shared with Sir Winston Churchill and she sent her friends copies of his book *Painting as a Pastime*. She began to collect paintings soon after she moved into Royal Lodge, buying an Augustus John and examples of Wilson Steer and Walter Sickert. Later she added works by Monet, Matthew Smith and Paul Nash. During her husband's lifetime, she asked John Piper to make watercolours and drawings of Windsor Castle. King George VI was traditional in his taste. Noticing that the sky was stormy, he commented drily, 'What bad weather you must have had, Mr Piper.'

The Queen Mother's final public appearance took place at Westminster Abbey where her royal life began on her marriage in 1923. While she was still in excellent health, with her usual common sense, she planned her own funeral down to the last detail. She occasionally popped into the Infirmary at the back of the Abbey to watch the ladies of St Faith, all voluntary and expert needlewomen, delicately repairing the Tudor roses on the royal funeral pall. And, with her exquisite good taste, she made one final request. 'I am afraid that I don't awfully care for your candles,' she told the Abbey's authorities. 'Do you mind if I bring my own?'

During her long and distinguished life the Queen Mother witnessed as many changes as the century she paralleled. When she was born, Queen Victoria was on the throne, people travelled by horse and carriage and the Boer War was still in full swing. Today Victoria's great-great granddaughter is Sovereign, people frequently travel by air, advertisements predict that holidays will soon be taken in space, and South Africa has black majority rule. She came through two world wars and witnessed the rise and fall of Communism. She saw the Court change beyond recognition and the world of her youth turned upside-down. Through all the trials and triumphs of her life she was the

Below: As regal as ever. Photographer Richard Stone captures that 'inner-beauty' which made the Queen Mother one of the most loved and admired figures of the twentieth century.

Right: On her ninety-eighth birthday the Queen Mother stands with friends and family outside Clarence House for the benefit of her admiring fans.

bed-rock on which the monarchy and the nation stood. She was the cornerstone of her family and the most adored grandmother in the land.

It is said that she once sent the Beefeaters at the Tower of London into a spin when she asked to borrow the Koh-I-Noor

Below: A portrait of the Queen Mother by Pietro Annigoni. He was to say that it was his best picture of her.

diamond, the largest gemstone in the world. But the Queen Mother needed no such embellishment. She was the jewel in the Crown, her magic undiminished even in old age. The royal portrait painter Pietro Annigoni was asked why one of his best pictures was of her. 'It's because she had such inner beauty,' he replied. 'The Queen Mother was one of the loveliest people I have ever met. It is hard to imagine a kinder, warmer, more appealing human being … She was absolutely perfect.' Her family, the nation and the world agreed.

Above and right: Elizabeth, the Queen Mother, sees the last of her grandchildren married. Prince Edward and Sophie Rhys-Jones, who became the Earl and Countess of Wessex, were married in St. George's Chapel, Windsor on 19 June 1999.

189

CHAPTER SEVEN

THE FINAL CHAPTER

Below: The Queen Mother visits Canisbay Church, which is close to the Castle of Mey, her home in the north of Scotland.

Opposite: On her 100th birthday, the Queen Mother looks radiant. This photograph was taken just before she received her birthday telegram outside Clarence House.

Queen Elizabeth, the Queen Mother, died much as she had lived – with dignity, grace and the minimum of fuss. Her end, like her life, showed the same pluck that she had displayed through thick and thin for over a century. Unlike her few critics, hard-bitten anti-monarchists for whom she could do no right, she was no whinger. For her, even in her last days, duty came first and self second. With the same valiant spirit that she had shown through the many tribulations that life threw at her, so she confronted death. For death was something that Queen Elizabeth had never feared. Her steadfast faith, learnt at her mother's knee and which had sustained her through the dark days of the abdication crisis, the Second World War and

her husband, King George VI's premature demise, kept as firm as ever as she prepared to meet her Maker. Her bravery had always been legendary and enabled her to shrug off the excruciating pain that necessitated two hip operations in her mid and late nineties and the constant discomfort of a leg ulcer that refused to heal. When most people half her age would have thrown in the towel, she went about her duties as if she had not a care in the world. No one to whom she chatted had the slightest inkling of the effort behind the twinkling blue eyes and golden smile as she mingled charmingly amongst her people. Once in a blue moon,

she did confess to occasionally getting slightly tired but quickly added that the affection that she got from the people she met, whatever walk of life they came from, 'recharges me. Gives me back my strength.'

Since she was a very small girl, Queen Elizabeth had professed that her favourite hobby was 'liking people' and it was a sentiment that grew with her as she got older. As a youngster, she was the friendly chatterbox who enchanted her parents' house guests and prompted one convalescent soldier, shattered by the horrors of First World War trench warfare, to say that he loved her quite as much as his 'fiancée'. As a debutante, she proved irresistible to men because of her compassion and warmth, a day never passing without the arrival of a secret billet-doux from one of her many admirers, passed on by a housemaid. King George V's younger son Bertie fell in love with her not because she was the prettiest girl of her generation but because she was the nicest and even his mother, the formidable Queen Mary, was charmed, declaring she was 'the one girl who could make Bertie happy.' She was not to be proved wrong. Her entry into the Royal Family brought her into the public eye and soon her *joie de vivre* and ability to make everyone she met feel the most special person in the world, earned the nickname 'The Smiling Duchess.' In America they dubbed her 'The Queen of Hearts', prompting President Roosevelt to remark to Bertie, 'My, you're a great Queen picker', and even the stony hearts of the Boers in South Africa, with long memories of their bloody conflict with Britain, melted when they turned out in their thousands to see her. In eighty years of public engagements, both at home and abroad, Queen Elizabeth was adored wherever she went, earning friends for not only herself but for the monarchy and the country.

Never was the love and esteem in which the Queen Mother was held better illustrated than during the 100th birthday pageant organised in her honour by the nation. Just sixteen days short of achieving her century and three days after beating the venerable

Queen Victoria by being the person to hold the title of Queen the longest, she braved the blazing heat of a July afternoon to watch 90 minutes of tributes and celebrations. Fittingly, it was a jolly affair, involving 7,000 people, a menagerie of animals and an enthusiastic audience of more than 12,000. Likened to the biggest village fête London had seen for a decade, the pageant began with a twenty-minute warm-up session as the massed bands, pipes and drums from British and Commonwealth military units strutted their stuff and played such old favourites as 'a Life on the Ocean Wave' to amuse the expectant crowd. The arrival of the guest of honour was heralded by trumpeters on the Admiralty roof as she suddenly appeared, surrounded by the Household Cavalry, on Horse Guards Parade. Resplendent in pink and flanked by the Prince of Wales, she acknowledged the roar of the crowd from her open landau as they broke out into spontaneous applause and began singing the National Anthem. The parade which followed, telling the story of the ten decades of the 20th century, was as colourful, whimsical and fun-loving as the Queen Mother was herself. Sitting on her dais, she seemed much amused when five members of the Worshipful Company of Grocers,

Above: Ballroom dancers were just one small part of the tributes and celebrations.

dressed in Tudor hats and fur-trimmed gowns, trotted into the arena on camels — one of the animals dropping deferentially to its knees as it passed her. Another highlight was the appearance of her corgis, Rush and Minnie, said by some to look a trifle overweight, who with her page William Tallon, led out a parade of the 300 organisations with which the Queen Mother has been associated. They ranged from the Girls Brigade to the AA to the Bembridge Lifeboat to the Hastings Winkle Club, who decided at the last minute to leave their winkles at home for fear that the heat might cause them to give offence. There were also stars a plenty including Sir Norman Wisdom representing the British film industry, the super model Jerry Hall dressed as the goddess Flora, stargazer Sir Patrick Moore, Dame Vera Lynn and 92-year-old Sir John Mills, who thanked her on behalf of the Commonwealth and the nation. A hundred white doves were released, a million rose petals fell and the Queen Mother was presented with a huge cake and giant birthday card bearing the signatures of all those who had taken part. As she said herself it had been a truly wonderful evening, adding, 'I hope you have enjoyed it as much as I have.'

Her birthday celebration, on 4 August 2000, was no less a triumph as 40,000 people gathered outside Buckingham Palace to roar their congratulations to the first member of the Royal Family to reach 100. During her five-minute appearance on the balcony, the scene of so many other historic events from VE Day to the wedding kiss of Prince Charles and Diana Spencer, she was joined by the Queen, Princess Margaret and 25 other members of the Royal Family.

Dressed in pale blue silk, she revelled in the crowd's attention as they sang 'Happy Birthday' and cheered their hearts out. Public adulation had always been her life's blood and that day was no

Above: One of the highlights of the Queen Mother's birthday pageant was the appearance of her corgis, Rush and Minni.

Right: HRH Queen Elizabeth and the rest of the Royal Family with the Queen Mother on the balcony of Buckingham Palace on the occasion of her 100th birthday.

different. As she acknowledged the crowd's affection, the years seemed to slip away as she stood sprightly, alert and full of happiness – like a woman thirty years younger.

Earlier in the day, the normal rituals that have marked so many birthdays swung into place. As usual Ivor Spencer and his Guild of Toastmasters arrived at Clarence House, her London home, with a nebuchadnezzar (twenty bottles) of champagne as flowers, greetings cards and birthday cakes arrived in delivery vans. Shortly before noon, the gates of Clarence House swung open and the Queen Mother emerged with Prince Charles at her side. The Queen's postman, newly arrived in his electric van, rushed forward to deliver one of twelve congratulatory messages sent by the Queen which her mother handed to her equerry to slit open the envelope with his ceremonial sword. Her daughter's personal message, in her own hand, read, 'On your 100th birthday, all the

Below: Crowds gather in front of Buckingham Palace to wish the Queen Mother a happy birthday.

Above: At Clarence House the Queen Mother reads her 100th birthday telegram from the Queen.

family join with me in sending you our love and best wishes for this special day'. She signed it with her pet childhood name, Lilibet.

Then in brilliant sunshine, thousands applauded as the Queen Mother made the ten-minute journey to Buckingham Palace in an open landau decorated with flowers in her racing colours of pale blue and gold. Some had been camped out for days to get the best vantage point on this very special day. As she entered the Palace gates the band of the Coldstream Guards played 'Congratulations' and 'Happy Birthday' as a giant Royal Standard, four times the normal size, fluttered overhead.

Prime Minister Tony Blair led the nation's congratulations and praised 'her extraordinary sense of duty, this sense of obligation to others which she has.' Other tributes poured in from countries around the world. President Putin of Russia praised her role in the Second World War and said that Stalingrad would never forget her support, while newspapers in America bore the banner headline 'Legend' over her photograph.

Meanwhile the Queen Mother was cheerfully eating her words as well as her cake. 'I'm not sure anyone will turn up,' she had replied when it was suggested that she appear on the Palace balcony on her birthday.

It was said that after her love for her late husband, King George VI, and her family, her greatest and most enduring passion was racing. To the end of her days, *The Sporting Post* was delivered every morning and it was to its crisp pages that she

Below: Prince Charles and the Queen Mother in an open landau on their journey from Clarence House to Buckingham Palace to continue her birthday celebrations.

turned first each day. What started out as a distraction, after the King died, became her main interest as the passing of the years meant that she had to abandon, but only in her eighties, her other great pleasure, fishing.

The Queen Mother regarded national hunt racing as 'proper' racing and could never understand why some people considered the Flat, more valuable in terms of prize money, as in any way superior. Characteristically, to her a cold, wet day at a jumps track, surrounded by people who were there for the sport rather than the glamour, was much more enjoyable than the fashionable Ascot meeting, populated by those who knew nothing about horses and were only present to see and be seen. The Queen Mother's interest in racing started in 1949 when her friend Lord Mildmay suggested that she should buy a chaser to take her mind off the worry of the King's health and to have some fun. In partnership with Princess Elizabeth, she followed his advice and the pair bought the eight-year-old Monaveen who, to their delight, won at his first start wearing the colours of the young Princess. The Queen Mother was hooked as was her daughter and, despite Monaveen's untimely death at a water jump, she registered her own colours, inherited from her racing-mad Strathmore kin.

She had early success with horses such as Manicou, Double Star and The Rip, but perhaps her most famous horse was Devon Loch. In the 1956 Grand National, just 100 yards from home and leading comfortably, he suddenly appeared to jump an imaginary fence and landed spread-eagled on the ground. His jockey, Dick Francis, who became a bestselling thriller writer and close friend of the Queen Mother, could only explain the horse's action by saying the roar of the crowd had put him off his stride. The Queen Mother was philosophical. 'That's racing', she remarked, although this was the closest she ever got to winning the National.

However, she did have other spectacular successes notably with Game Spirit, who won 21 races, and Special Cargo, who won the Whitbread Gold Cup by a whisker leading the Queen Mother

Above: The Queen and the Queen Mother look on after the finish of the annual Epsom Derby in June 2000.

to receive the very same trophy she had agreed to present. In her last years, Queen Elizabeth took great delight in breeding her own horses on the Sandringham estate and was full of plans for her foals, four or five years hence, at the time of her death. She was spurred on when her homebred horse Double Brandy romped home in the summer of 1999, outstripping hugely expensive thoroughbreds, and giving her her first victory on the Flat for forty years. Even though Queen Elizabeth never felt herself old – and often made remarks like 'I must go over and speak to those poor old folks over there', when in fact they were twenty or thirty years younger than herself – she did eventually have to make a concession in order to enjoy her racing to the full. When most people would have been content to sit in the royal box and watch the race on television, she always insisted on seeing the horses for herself in the paddock. With a perfect combination of humour and dignity, she took to taking a golf buggy, decked out in her colours of pale blue and buff with a black bobble and gold tassel on the roof, to see the runners and riders. Her ladies-in-waiting struggled to keep up with the speedy great-Grannie.

Queen Elizabeth, The Queen Mother, died peacefully in her sleep on the afternoon of Easter Saturday, 30 March 2002, at her Windsor home, Royal Lodge, as the Queen sat at her bedside gently holding her hand. She was 101 years and 238 days old. Her death at 3.15 pm came after a long struggle against a chest infection which she had been fighting since Christmas and seven weeks after the death of her younger daughter, Princess Margaret, aged 71. Her last public appearance was at her daughter's funeral when, as stalwart as ever, she defied doctors' advice to attend the Windsor ceremony, held on the 50th anniversary of the funeral of her late husband, King George VI.

The Queen was out riding in the Windsor Castle grounds when she was alerted by doctors that her mother was about to die and she returned as quickly as possible. The local clergyman was called to the bedside and he was able to say prayers and sign the cross on the Queen Mother's forehead before she passed away. Alongside her two doctors, Princess Margaret's recently bereaved children, Viscount Linley and Lady Sarah Chatto, were also present as was Queen Elizabeth's niece, The Honourable Mrs. Margaret Rhodes, who described the moment as 'extraordinarily emotional and very moving'. She added, 'It was wonderfully peaceful because Queen Elizabeth became unconscious. It was just rather agonizing waiting. The Queen went away to get out of her riding clothes. She came back … The moment of death was peaceful. She just slipped away. There is an element of relief, isn't there? One is glad for them. It's over … My aunt had a wonderful life. Filled to the brim. And if anybody is perfectly sure of being greeted by St. Peter straight away, it's Queen Elizabeth.'

Prince Charles, who had last seen his grandmother two days earlier prior to a skiing holiday in Switzerland with his sons Prince William and Prince Harry, was told soon after by the Queen and was said to be 'heartbroken'. Within minutes of the announcement of her death, crowds began to gather at Buckingham Palace, Windsor Castle and her London home, Clarence House, and police had to put up barriers as the flood of floral tributes poured in. The Palace flag was lowered to half-mast and books of condolence were opened. Hundreds of thousands signed them and tens of thousands filed past her coffin to say a final farewell.

The Queen Mother had seemed to be on the mend and just ten days before her death, disappointed at missing the Cheltenham meeting, she held a cocktail party for her horse racing friends and talked about how much she was looking forward to taking part in the Queen's Golden Jubilee celebrations. But, in her final days, sensing that the end was near, she uncharacteristically shunned company and increasingly locked herself away. In long conversations with the Queen, she reminisced about her life, talking particularly of the late King and Princess Margaret, and, in a poignant gesture, gave presents to close members of her family.

As the Queen and the nation began nine days of mourning, the Queen Mother began her final journey. Under leaden skies,

Below: The Queen watches as pallbearers carry the coffin into Westminster Hall after the ceremonial procession from the Queen's Chapel in St. James's Palace.

her coffin, draped in her personal royal standard and bearing a single wreath of pink camellias picked that morning from her own beloved garden, was carried by six pallbearers to the small Royal Chapel of All Saints in Windsor Great Park, where she had worshipped for seven decades. There 16 members of the Royal Family, including Prince Andrew and his daughters Princesses Beatrice and Eugenie who had flown back from a holiday in the Bahamas, attended a private evensong requested by the Queen in her mother's memory. Most seemed close to tears as they left.

The next day the coffin was taken by road to the Queen's Chapel in St. James's Palace, where the coffin of Princess Margaret had rested only 49 days earlier, in order that the family and the Queen Mother's staff might pay their private respects. MPs and peers gathered at the Houses of Parliament to pay their tributes. After a minutes silence during a special session of the Commons, recalled from the Easter break, Prime Minister Tony Blair spoke of how the Queen Mother spanned the generations and the vast

Below: The Queen Mother's grandsons, Prince Charles, Prince Andrew, Prince Edward and Viscount Linley, mount a vigil around her coffin as it lies in state in Westminster Hall.

sweep of history. 'It is the spirit of duty that captures her spirit best,' he said. 'It is that combination of integrity and simple humanity that made her not just respected, but loved.' Prince Charles, in his own moving tribute, described the Queen Mother as his 'darling, magical grandmother.' Prince William fondly recalled her impersonations of television star Ali G, which had the whole family in stitches, adding: 'I remember her as being a huge inspiration to me, someone to really look up to and admire. She was a historic link.'

Six days after her death, the Queen Mother was borne to her lying-in-state at Westminster Hall in a ceremonial procession watched by a crowd of 400,000. At 11.30 am the first gun of the 28-gun salute was fired and the military bands started playing Beethoven's *Funeral March*. As one, the 1,600 servicemen and women in the procession moved off, their rifles and swords reversed, as the cortege began its mile long journey.

On the coffin was placed a single wreath of white roses, sweet peas and freesias from the Queen, with the hand-written message, 'In loving memory, Lilibet', her mother's pet name for her daughter. Beside it, on a velvet cushion, sat the platinum crown with its 2,800 diamonds topped by the priceless Koh-i-Noor, which she had worn for King George VI's Coronation in 1937.

Three generations of the Royal family, including, by special dispensation, Princess Anne, and members of the Bowes Lyon family walked behind the horse-drawn gun carriage as it made its way in hazy sunshine from St. James's Palace before halting, to public applause, in front of the North Door. As Big Ben struck noon, the coffin was carried into Westminster Hall to the catafalque. The Royal Family, led by the Queen and Prince Philip, followed and, after short prayers, the first vigil was mounted. It

Above: Princess Anne, the Duke of Edinburgh, Prince Charles and Prince Andrew walking behind the coffin of the Queen Mother during the ceremonial procession to Westminster Hall on 5 April 2002.

was the moment that Prince Charles finally succumbed to the tears he had fought back during the 28 minute procession.

On the eve of the funeral, the Queen addressed the nation in a televised broadcast from Windsor Castle thanking her people for the support they had given the Royal Family and the love and honour they had given her mother in death. She emphasized her mother's 'infectious zest for living' and hoped that sadness would blend with 'a wider sense of thanksgiving' at her funeral.

As the message went out, the Queen Mother's four grandsons mounted a 20 minute Vigil of the Watch around her coffin, echoing the tribute paid at King George V's lying-in-state by his four sons 66 years earlier. They were silently watched by other members of the Royal Family and Camilla Parker Bowles, Prince Charles's companion, who also attended the funeral.

On the chilly spring morning of April 9 the Queen Mother's body was borne by gun-carriage to Westminster Abbey for her funeral as the massed bands of the pipes and drums played *My Home* and 400,000 well-wishers, some who had camped out overnight, looked on. Members of the Royal Family and the Bowes Lyon family again walked behind the coffin before the hour-long ecumenical service which included some of the Queen

Mother's favourites – Psalm 121, *I will lift up mine eyes unto the hills* and the hymn *Immortal, invisible God only wise*. Throughout the country a two-minute silence was observed as she arrived, at 11.30 am, at the Abbey where she was married and crowned Queen.

As her crown glinted in the candlelight and Prince Charles, rigid with grief, silently wept for his grandmother, the Archbishop of Canterbury Dr. George Carey spoke of the Queen Mother's strength, dignity and laughter ending with a quote from the Book of Proverbs, 'Many have done excellently but you exceed them all.' After the last post was sounded and the National Anthem sung, the Queen Mother's coffin was transferred to a hearse as the band played an Irish lament. It was driven slowly through London and down to St. George's Chapel, Windsor, where she was buried at a private family service with the late King George VI, and the ashes of her beloved daughter Princess Margaret. More than a million people lined the route, showering her hearse with flowers, conscious that they will not see her like again.

Above: Britain's Royal Family look towards the coffin of the Queen Mother during her funeral service inside Westminster Abbey on 9 April 2002.

INDEX

ACKNOWLEDGEMENTS

The photographs listed below are protected by copyright.

CECIL BEATON: 69 (top right and centre), 73, 83, 89 (centre), 114, 117, 174.

CAMERA PRESS: half title, frontispiece, 8, 9, 13, 14, 15, 16, 19, 20, 24, 25 (both), 38, 39, 40, 41, 47, 48, 49 (top), 51, 52 (bottom), 53, 54 (top), 60, 61, 63, 64, 65 (bottom), 66, 68 (top left, centre, bottom left), 69 (top right and centre), 73, 74, 77, 79, 83, 84 (both), 85, 87, 89 (centre and bottom), 92 (bottom), 93, 94, 96, 98, 99, 101, 107, 108, 112, 113, 114, 115, 117, 118, 119, 124 (top centre and bottom), 125 (top and bottom), 126, 128, 129, 130, 131, 132, 133, 135, 136, 137, 138, 139, 141, 142 (both), 144 (both), 145 (both), 147, 150, 151 (both), 152 (top), 153, 154, 155, 156, 157, 158, 160 (both), 163, 164, 166, 167, 168 (top), 169 (bottom), 171 (both), 172, 174, 176 (bottom), 179, 180 (bottom), 181, 183 (top), 184 (both), 185, 186, 187, 188 (both), 189 (both), 190, 191, 193, 194, 195 (both), 196, 197 (both).

ANTHONY CRICKMAY: 167.

ET ARCHIVE: 80 (bottom).

EXPRESS NEWSPAPERS: 97, 105, 111 (both), 162 (both), 170, 173, 182.

JOHN FROST NEWSPAPERS: 32 (top), 88 (bottom), 124 (top left), 125 (centre), 149 (centre), 176 (top right).

GLAMIS: 17, 34, 35, 36, 37, 148 (top right).

HULTON GETTY: 33 (top), 68 (top right), 148 (top left).

ILLUSTRATED LONDON NEWS: 18, 23, 26, 27, 29, 31, 43, 45, 49 (bottom), 50 (both), 52 (top), 54 (bottom), 55, 56, 57, 59, 65 (top), 69 (bottom), 71, 75, 80 (top), 82, 86, 87, 88 (top and centre), 89 (top), 90, 91, 92 (top), 100, 110, 140, 159, 161, 183 (bottom).

PATRICK LICHFIELD: 129.

DESMOND O'NEILL: 121.

PA NEWS: 7, 148 (bottom), 162 (top), 176 (top left and centre), 177 (top and centre), 180 (top).

SNOWDON: 181.

TOPHAM: 11, 12, 32, 33 (centre and bottom), 62, 102, 103, 109, 123, 124 (top right), 134, 143, 148 (centre), 149 (top and bottom), 152 (bottom), 165, 168 (bottom), 177 (bottom).

REUTERS NEWS PICTURE SERVICE: 199, 201, 202, 203, 204, 205.

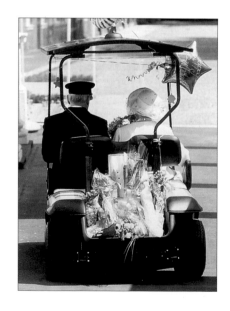